MYTHS
AND FOLK TALES
OF IRELAND

JEREMIAH CURTIN

MYTHS
AND FOLK TALES
OF IRELAND

DOVER PUBLICATIONS, INC.
NEW YORK

Published in Canada by General Publishing Company, Ltd., 30 Lesmill Road, Don Mills, Toronto, Ontario.

Published in the United Kingdom by Constable and Company, Ltd., 10 Orange Street, London WC 2.

This Dover edition, first published in 1975, is an unabridged republication of the work originally published in Boston by Little, Brown and Company in 1890 under the title *Myths and Folk-Lore of Ireland*. None of the stories have been abridged, but the introduction, frontispiece, and dedication of the original edition have been omitted from this Dover edition.

International Standard Book Number: 0-486-22430-9
Library of Congress Catalog Card Number: 69-18206

Manufactured in the United States of America
Dover Publications, Inc.
180 Varick Street
New York, N.Y. 10014

CONTENTS.

MYTHS
AND FOLK TALES
OF IRELAND

THE SON OF THE KING OF ERIN AND THE GIANT OF LOCH LÉIN.[1]

ON a time there lived a king and a queen in Erin, and they had an only son. They were very careful and fond of this son; whatever he asked for was granted, and what he wanted he had.

When grown to be almost a young man the son went away one day to the hills to hunt. He could find no game, — saw nothing all day. Towards evening he sat down on a hillside to rest, but soon stood up again and started to go home empty-handed. Then he heard a whistle behind him, and turning, saw a giant hurrying down the hill.

The giant came to him, took his hand, and said: "Can you play cards?"

"I can indeed," said the king's son.

"Well, if you can," said the giant, "we'll have a game here on this hillside."

So the two sat down, and the giant had out a pack of cards in a twinkling. "What shall we play for?" asked the giant.

"For two estates," answered the king's son.

They played: the young man won, and went home the better for two estates. He was very glad, and hurried to tell his father the luck he had.

Next day he went to the same place, and didn't wait long till the giant came again.

"Welcome, king's son," said the giant. "What shall we play for to-day?"

[1] Loch Léin, former name of one of the Lakes of Killarney.

" I 'll leave that to yourself," answered the young man.

"Well," said the giant, " I have five hundred bullocks with golden horns and silver hoofs, and I 'll play them against as many cattle belonging to you."

" Agreed," said the king's son.

They played. The giant lost again. He had the cattle brought to the place; and the king's son went home with the five hundred bullocks. The king his father was outside watching, and was more delighted than the day before when he saw the drove of beautiful cattle with horns of gold and hoofs of silver.

When the bullocks were driven in, the king sent for the old blind sage (Sean dall Glic), to know what he would say of the young man's luck.

" My advice," said the old blind sage, " is not to let your son go the way of the giant again, for if he plays with him a third time he 'll rue it."

But nothing could keep the king's son from playing the third time. Away he went, in spite of every advice and warning, and sat on the same hillside.

He waited long, but no one came. At last he rose to go home. That moment he heard a whistle behind him, and turning, saw the giant coming.

" Well, will you play with me to-day? " asked the giant.

" I would," said the king's son, " but I have nothing to bet."

" You have indeed."

" I have not," said the king's son.

" Haven't you your head? " asked the giant of Loch Léin, for it was he that was in it.

" I have," answered the king's son.

"So have I my head," said the giant; "and we'll play for each other's heads."

This third time the giant won the game; and the king's son was to give himself up in a year and a day to the giant in his castle.

The young man went home sad and weary. The king and queen were outside watching, and when they saw him approaching, they knew great trouble was on him. When he came to where they were, he would n't speak, but went straight into the castle, and would n't eat or drink.

He was sad and lamenting for a good while, till at last he disappeared one day, the king and queen knew not whither. After that they did n't hear of him, — did n't know was he dead or alive.

The young man after he left home was walking along over the kingdom for a long time. One day he saw no house, big or little, till after dark he came in front of a hill, and at the foot of the hill saw a small light. He went to the light, found a small house, and inside an old woman sitting at a warm fire, and every tooth in her head as long as a staff.

She stood up when he entered, took him by the hand, and said, "You are welcome to my house, son of the king of Erin." Then she brought warm water, washed his feet and legs from the knees down, gave him supper, and put him to bed.

When he rose next morning he found breakfast ready before him. The old woman said: "You were with me last night; you'll be with my sister to-night, and what she tells you to do, do, or your head'll be in danger. Now take the gift I give you. Here is a ball of thread: do you throw it in front of you before you start, and all day the ball will be rolling ahead of you, and you'll be following behind winding the thread into another ball."

He obeyed the old woman, threw the ball down, and followed. All the day he was going up hill and down, across valleys and open places, keeping the ball in sight and winding the thread as he went, till evening, when he saw a hill in front, and a small light at the foot of it.

He went to the light and found a house, which he entered. There was no one inside but an old woman with teeth as long as a crutch.

"Oh! then you are welcome to my house, king's son of Erin," said she. "You were with my sister last night; you are with me to-night; and it's glad I am to see you."

She gave him meat and drink and a good bed to lie on.

When he rose next morning breakfast was there before him, and when he had eaten and was ready for the journey, the old woman gave him a ball of thread, saying: "You were with my younger sister the night before last; you were with me last night; and you'll be with my elder sister to-night. You must do what she tells you, or you'll lose your head. You must throw this ball before you, and follow the clew till evening."

He threw down the ball: it rolled on, showing the way up and down mountains and hills, across valleys and braes. All day he wound the ball; unceasingly it went till nightfall, when he came to a light, found a little house, and went in. Inside was an old woman, the eldest sister, who said: "You are welcome, and glad am I to see you, king's son."

She treated him as well as the other two had done. After he had eaten breakfast next morning, she said : —

"I know well the journey you are on. You

have lost your head to the Giant of Loch Léin, and
you are going to give yourself up.   This giant has
a great castle.   Around the castle are seven hundred iron spikes, and on every spike of them but
one is the head of a king, a queen, or a king's son.
The seven hundredth spike is empty, and nothing
can save your head from that spike if you don't
take my advice.

" Here is a ball for you: walk behind it till you
come to a lake near the giant's castle.   When
you come to that lake at midday the ball will be
unwound.

" The giant has three young daughters, and they
come at noon every day of the year to bathe in the
lake.   You must watch them well, for each will
have a lily on her breast, — one a blue, another a
white, and the third a yellow lily.   You must n't
let your eyes off the one with the yellow lily.
Watch her well: when she undresses to go into the
water, see where she puts her clothes; when the
three are out in the lake swimming, do you slip
away with the clothes of Yellow Lily.

" When the sisters come out from bathing, and
find that the one with the yellow lily has lost her
clothes, the other two will laugh and make game
of her, and she will crouch down crying on the
shore, with nothing to cover her, and say, ' How
can I go home now, and everybody making sport
of me?   Whoever took my clothes, if he 'll give
them back to me, I 'll save him from the danger he
is in, if I have the power.' "

The king's son followed the ball till nearly noon,
when it stopped at a lake not far from the giant's
castle.   Then he hid behind a rock at the water's
edge, and waited.

At midday the three sisters came to the lake,

and, leaving their clothes on the strand, went into the water. When all three were in the lake swimming and playing with great pleasure and sport, the king's son slipped out and took the clothes of the sister with the yellow lily.

After they had bathed in the lake to their hearts' content, the three sisters came out. When the two with the blue and the white lilies saw their sister on the shore and her clothes gone, they began to laugh and make sport of her. Then, cowering and crouching down, she began to cry and lament, saying: " How can I go home now, with my own sisters laughing at me? If I stir from this, everybody will see me and make sport of me."

The sisters went home and left her there. When they were gone, and she was alone at the water crying and sobbing, all at once she came to herself and called out: "Whoever took my clothes, I 'll forgive him if he brings them to me now, and I 'll save him from the danger he is in if I can."

When he heard this, the king's son put the clothes out to her, and stayed behind himself till she told him to come forth.

Then she said: " I know well where you are going. My father, the Giant of Loch Léin, has a soft bed waiting for you, — a deep tank of water for your death. But don't be uneasy; go into the water, and wait till I come to save you. Be at that castle above before my father. When he comes home to-night and asks for you, take no meat from him, but go to rest in the tank when he tells you."

The giant's daughter left the king's son, who went his way to the castle alone at a fair and easy gait, for he had time enough on his hands and to spare.

When the Giant of Loch Léin came home that night, the first question he asked was, " Is the son of the king of Erin here? "

" I am," said the king's son.

" Come," said the giant, " and get your evening's meat."

" I 'll take no meat now, for I don't need it," said the king's son.

"Well, come with me then, and I 'll show you your bed." He went, and the giant put the king's son into the deep tank of water to drown, and being tired himself from hunting all day over the mountains and hills of Erin, he went to sleep.

That minute his youngest daughter came, took the king's son out of the tank, placed plenty to eat and to drink before him, and gave him a good bed to sleep on that night.

The giant's daughter watched till she heard her father stirring before daybreak; then she roused the king's son, and put him in the tank again.

Soon the giant came to the tank and called out: " Are you here, son of the king of Erin? "

" I am," said the king's son.

" Well, come out now. There is a great work for you to-day. I have a stable outside, in which I keep five hundred horses, and that stable has not been cleaned these seven hundred years. My great-grandmother when a girl lost a slumber-pin (*bar an suan*) somewhere in that stable, and never could find it. You must have that pin for me when I come home to-night; if you don't, your head will be on the seven hundredth spike to-morrow."

Then two shovels were brought for him to choose

from to clean out the stable, an old and a new one. He chose the new shovel, and went to work.

For every shovelful he threw out, two came in; and soon the door of the stable was closed on him. When the stable-door was closed, the giant's daughter called from outside: " How are you thriving now, king's son? "

" I 'm not thriving at all," said the king's son; " for as much as I throw out, twice as much comes in, and the door is closed against me."

" You must make a way for me to come in, and I 'll help you," said she.

" How can I do that? " asked the king's son.

However, she did it. The giant's daughter made her way into the stable, and she was n't long inside till the stable was cleared, and she saw the *bar an suan.*

" There is the pin over there in the corner," said she to the king's son, who put it in his bosom to give to the giant.

Now he was happy, and the giant's daughter had good meat and drink put before him.

When the giant himself came home, he asked: " How did you do your work to-day? "

" I did it well; I thought nothing of it."

" Did you find the *bar an suan?* "

" I did indeed; here 't is for you."

" Oh! then," said the giant, " it is either the devil or my daughter that helped you to do that work, for I know you never did it alone."

" It 's neither the devil nor your daughter, but my own strength that did the work," said the son of the king of Erin.

" You have done the work; now you must have your meat."

" I want no meat to-day; I am well satisfied as I am," said the king's son.

" Well," said the giant, " since you'll have no meat, you must go to sleep in the tank."

He went into the tank. The giant himself was soon snoring, for he was tired from hunting over Erin all day.

The moment her father was away, Yellow Lily came, took the king's son out of the tank, gave him a good supper and bed, and watched till the giant was stirring before daybreak. Then she roused the king's son and put him in the tank.

" Are you alive in the tank? " asked the giant at daybreak.

" I am," said the king's son.

" Well, you have a great work before you to-day. That stable you cleaned yesterday hasn't been thatched these seven hundred years, and if you don't have it thatched for me when I come home to-night, with birds' feathers, and not two feathers of one color or kind, I'll have your head on the seven hundredth spike to-morrow."

" Here are two whistles, — an old, and a new one; take your choice of them to call the birds."

The king's son took the new whistle, and set out over the hills and valleys, whistling as he went. But no matter how he whistled, not a bird came near him. At last, tired and worn out with travelling and whistling, he sat down on a hillock and began to cry.

That moment Yellow Lily was at his side with a cloth, which she spread out, and there was a grand meal before him. He hadn't finished eating and drinking, before the stable was thatched with birds' feathers, and no two of them of one color or kind.

When he came home that evening the giant

called out: " Have you the stable thatched for me to-night? "

" I have indeed," said the king's son; " and small trouble I had with it."

" If that's true," said the giant, " either the devil or my daughter helped you."

" It was my own strength, and not the devil or your daughter that helped me," said the king's son.

He spent that night as he had the two nights before.

Next morning, when the giant found him alive in the tank, he said: " There is great work before you to-day, which you must do, or your head 'll be on the spike to-morrow. Below here, under my castle, is a tree nine hundred feet high, and there isn't a limb on that tree, from the roots up, except one small limb at the very top, where there is a crow's nest. The tree is covered with glass from the ground to the crow's nest. In the nest is one egg: you must have that egg before me here for my supper to-night, or I 'll have your head on the seven hundredth spike to-morrow."

The giant went hunting, and the king's son went down to the tree, tried to shake it, but could not make it stir. Then he tried to climb; but no use, it was all slippery glass. Then he thought, " Sure I 'm done for now; I must lose my head this time."

He stood there in sadness, when Yellow Lily came, and said: " How are you thriving in your work? "

" I can do nothing," said the king's son.

" Well, all that we have done up to this time is nothing to climbing this tree. But first of all let us sit down together and eat, and then we 'll talk," said Yellow Lily.

They sat down, she spread the cloth again, and

they had a splendid feast. When the feast was
over she took out a knife from her pocket and
said : —

" Now you must kill me, strip the flesh from my
bones, take all the bones apart, and use them as
steps for climbing the tree. When you are climbing the tree, they will stick to the glass as if they
had grown out of it; but when you are coming
down, and have put your foot on each one, they will
drop into your hand when you touch them. Be
sure and stand on each bone, leave none untouched;
if you do, it will stay behind. Put all my flesh into
this clean cloth by the side of the spring at the
roots of the tree. When you come to the earth,
arrange my bones together, put the flesh over
them, sprinkle it with water from the spring, and
I shall be alive and well before you. But don't
forget a bone of me on the tree."

" How could I kill you," asked the king's son,
" after what you have done for me ? "

" If you won't obey, you and I are done for,"
said Yellow Lily. " You must climb the tree, or
we are lost; and to climb the tree you must do as
I say."

The king's son obeyed. He killed Yellow Lily,
cut the flesh from her body, and unjointed the
bones, as she had told him.

As he went up, the king's son put the bones of
Yellow Lily's body against the side of the tree,
using them as steps, till he came under the nest
and stood on the last bone.

Then he took the crow's egg; and coming down,
put his foot on every bone, then took it with him,
till he came to the last bone, which was so near
the ground that he failed to touch it with his
foot.

He now placed all the bones of Yellow Lily in

order again at the side of the spring, put the flesh on them, sprinkled it with water from the spring. She rose up before him, and said: "Did n't I tell you not to leave a bone of my body without stepping on it? Now I am lame for life! You left my little toe on the tree without touching it, and I have but nine toes."

When the giant came home that night, the first words he had were, "Have you the crow's egg for my supper?"

"I have," said the king's son.

"If you have, then either the devil or my daughter is helping you."

"It is my own strength that 's helping me," said the king's son.

"Well, whoever it is, I must forgive you now, and your head is your own."

So the king's son was free to go his own road, and away he went, and never stopped till he came home to his own father and mother, who had a great welcome before him; and why not? for they thought he was dead.

When the son was at home a time, the king called up the old blind sage, and asked, "What must I do with my son now?"

"If you follow my advice," said the old blind sage, "you 'll find a wife for him; and then he 'll not go roaming away again, and leave you as he did before."

The king was pleased with the advice, and he sent a message to the king of Lochlin [1] to ask his daughter in marriage.

The king of Lochlin came with the daughter and a ship full of attendants, and there was to be a grand wedding at the castle of the king of Erin.

[1] Lochlin, — Denmark.

Now, the king's son asked his father to invite the Giant of Loch Léin and Yellow Lily to the wedding. The king sent messages for them to come.

The day before the marriage there was a great feast at the castle. As the feast went on, and all were merry, the Giant of Loch Léin said: " I never was at a place like this but one man sang a song, a second told a story, and the third played a trick."

Then the king of Erin sang a song, the king of Lochlin told a story, and when the turn came to the giant, he asked Yellow Lily to take his place.

She threw two grains of wheat in the air, and there came down on the table two pigeons. The cock pigeon pecked at the hen and pushed her off the table. Then the hen called out to him in a human voice, " You would n't do that to me the day I cleaned the stable for you."

Next time Yellow Lily put two grains of wheat on the table. The cock ate the wheat, pecked the hen, and pushed her off the table to the floor. The hen said: " You would not do that to me the day I thatched the stable for you with birds' feathers, and not two of one color or kind."

The third time Yellow Lily put two more grains of wheat on the table. The cock ate both, and pushed the hen off to the floor. Then the hen called out: " You would n't do that to me the day you killed me and took my bones to make steps up the glass tree nine hundred feet high to get the crow's egg for the supper of the Giant of Loch Léin, and forget my little toe when you were coming down, and left me lame for life."

" Well," said the king's son to the guests at the

feast, " when I was a little younger than I am now, I used to be everywhere in the world sporting and gaming; and once when I was away, I lost the key of a casket that I had. I had a new key made, and after it was brought to me I found the old one. Now, I'll leave it to any one here to tell what am I to do, — which of the keys should I keep?"

"My advice to you," said the king of Lochlin, " is to keep the old key, for it fits the lock better, and you 're more used to it."

Then the king's son stood up and said: " I thank you, king of Lochlin, for a wise advice and an honest word. This is my bride, the daughter of the Giant of Loch Léin. I'll have her, and no other woman. Your daughter is my father's guest, and no worse, but better, for having come to a wedding in Erin."

The king's son married Yellow Lily, daughter of the Giant of Loch Léin, the wedding lasted long, and all were happy.

THE THREE DAUGHTERS OF KING O'HARA.

THERE was a king in Desmond whose name was Coluath O'Hara, and he had three daughters. On a time when the king was away from home, the eldest daughter took a thought that she 'd like to be married. So she went up in the castle, put on the cloak of darkness which her father had, and wished for the most beautiful man under the sun as a husband for herself.

She got her wish; for scarcely had she put off the cloak of darkness, when there came, in a golden coach with four horses, two black and two white, the finest man she had ever laid eyes on, and took her away.

When the second daughter saw what had happened to her sister, she put on the cloak of darkness, and wished for the next best man in the world as a husband.

She put off the cloak; and straightway there came, in a golden coach with four black horses, a man nearly as good as the first, and took her away.

The third sister put on the cloak, and wished for the best white dog in the world.

Presently he came, with one man attending, in a golden coach and four snow-white horses, and took the youngest sister away.

When the king came home, the stable-boy told him what had happened while he was gone. He was enraged beyond measure when he heard that his youngest daughter had wished for a white dog, and gone off with him.

When the first man brought his wife home he asked: "In what form will you have me in the daytime, — as I am now in the daytime, or as I am now at night?"

"As you are now in the daytime."

So the first sister had her husband as a man in the daytime; but at night he was a seal.

The second man put the same question to the middle sister, and got the same answer; so the second sister had her husband in the same form as the first.

When the third sister came to where the white dog lived, he asked her: "How will you have me to be in the daytime, — as I am now in the day, or as I am now at night?"

"As you are now in the day."

So the white dog was a dog in the daytime, but the most beautiful of men at night.

After a time the third sister had a son; and one day, when her husband was going out to hunt, he warned her that if anything should happen the child, not to shed a tear on that account.

While he was gone, a great gray crow that used to haunt the place came and carried the child away when it was a week old.

Remembering the warning, she shed not a tear for the loss.

All went on as before till another son was born. The husband used to go hunting every day, and again he said she must not shed a tear if anything happened.

When the child was a week old a great gray

crow came and bore him away; but the mother did not cry or drop a tear.

All went well till a daughter was born. When she was a week old a great gray crow came and swept her away. This time the mother dropped one tear on a handkerchief, which she took out of her pocket, and then put back again.

When the husband came home from hunting and heard what the crow had done, he asked the wife, "Have you shed tears this time?"

"I have dropped one tear," said she.

Then he was very angry; for he knew what harm she had done by dropping that one tear.

Soon after their father invited the three sisters to visit him and be present at a great feast in their honor. They sent messages, each from her own place, that they would come.

The king was very glad at the prospect of seeing his children; but the queen was grieved, and thought it a great disgrace that her youngest daughter had no one to come home with her but a white dog.

The white dog was in dread that the king wouldn't leave him inside with the company, but would drive him from the castle to the yard, and that the dogs outside wouldn't leave a patch of skin on his back, but would tear the life out of him.

The youngest daughter comforted him. "There is no danger to you," said she, "for wherever I am, you'll be, and wherever you go, I'll follow and take care of you."

When all was ready for the feast at the castle, and the company were assembled, the king was for banishing the white dog; but the youngest daughter would not listen to her father, — would not let the white dog out of her sight, but kept him near her at the feast, and divided with him the food that came to herself.

When the feast was over, and all the guests had gone, the three sisters went to their own rooms in the castle.

Late in the evening the queen took the cook with her, and stole in to see what was in her daughters' rooms. They were all asleep at the time. What should she see by the side of her youngest daughter but the most beautiful man she had ever laid eyes on.

Then she went to where the other two daughters were sleeping; and there, instead of the two men who brought them to the feast, were two seals, fast asleep.

The queen was greatly troubled at the sight of the seals. When she and the cook were returning, they came upon the skin of the white dog. She caught it up as she went, and threw it into the kitchen fire.

The skin was not five minutes in the fire when it gave a crack that woke not only all in the castle, but all in the country for miles around.

The husband of the youngest daughter sprang up. He was very angry and very sorry, and said: "If I had been able to spend three nights with you under your father's roof, I should have got back my own form again for good, and could have been a man both in the day and the night; but now I must go."

He rose from the bed, ran out of the castle, and away he went as fast as ever his two legs could carry him, overtaking the one before him, and leaving the one behind. He was this way all that night and the next day; but he could n't leave the wife, for she followed from the castle, was after him in the night and the day too, and never lost sight of him.

In the afternoon he turned, and told her to go
back to her father; but she would not listen to him.
At nightfall they came to the first house they had
seen since leaving the castle. He turned and said:
" Do you go inside and stay in this house till morning; I 'll pass the night outside where I am."

The wife went in. The woman of the house rose
up, gave her a pleasant welcome, and put a good
supper before her. She was not long in the house
when a little boy came to her knee and called her
" mother."

The woman of the house told the child to go
back to his place, and not to come out again.

" Here are a pair of scissors," said the woman of
the house to the king's daughter, " and they will
serve you well. Whatever ragged people you see,
if you cut a piece off their rags, that moment they
will have new clothes of cloth of gold."

She stayed that night, for she had good welcome.
Next morning when she went out, her husband
said: " You 'd better go home now to your
father."

" I 'll not go to my father if I have to leave
you," said she.

So he went on, and she followed. It was that
way all the day till night came; and at nightfall
they saw another house at the foot of a hill, and
again the husband stopped and said: " You go in;
I 'll stop outside till morning."

The woman of the house gave her a good welcome. After she had eaten and drunk, a little boy
came out of another room, ran to her knee, and
said, " Mother." The woman of the house sent the
boy back to where he had come from, and told him
to stay there.

Next morning, when the princess was going out
to her husband, the woman of the house gave her a

comb, and said: " If you meet any person with a diseased and a sore head, and draw this comb over it three times, the head will be well, and covered with the most beautiful golden hair ever seen."

She took the comb, and went out to her husband.

" Leave me now," said he, "and go back to your own father."

" I will not," said she, " but I will follow you while I have the power." So they went forward that day, as on the other two.

At nightfall they came to a third house, at the foot of a hill, where the princess received a good welcome. After she had eaten supper, a little girl with only one eye came to her knee and said, " Mother."

The princess began to cry at sight of the child, thinking that she herself was the cause that it had but one eye. Then she put her hand into her pocket where she kept the handkerchief on which she had dropped the tear when the gray crow carried her infant away. She had never used the handkerchief since that day, for there was an eye on it.

She opened the handkerchief, and put the eye in the girl's head. It grew into the socket that minute, and the child saw out of it as well as out of the other eye; and then the woman of the house sent the little one to bed.

Next morning, as the king's daughter was going out, the woman of the house gave her a whistle, and said: " Whenever you put this whistle to your mouth and blow on it, all the birds of the air will come to you from every quarter under the sun. Be careful of the whistle, as it may serve you greatly."

" Go back to your father's castle," said the husband when she came to him, " for I must leave you to-day."

They went on together a few hundred yards, and then sat on a green hillock, and he told the wife: " Your mother has come between us; but for her we might have lived together all our days. If I had been allowed to pass three nights with you in your father's house, I should have got back my form of a man both in the daytime and the night. The Queen of Tir na n-Og [the land of youth] enchanted and put on me a spell, that unless I could spend three nights with a wife under her father's roof in Erin, I should bear the form of a white dog one half of my time; but if the skin of the dog should be burned before the three nights were over, I must go down to her kingdom and marry the queen herself. And 't is to her I am going to-day. I have no power to stay, and I must leave you; so farewell, you 'll never see me again on the upper earth."

He left her sitting on the mound, went a few steps forward to some bulrushes, pulled up one, and disappeared in the opening where the rush had been.

She stopped there, sitting on the mound lamenting, till evening, not knowing what to do. At last she bethought herself, and going to the rushes, pulled up a stalk, went down, followed her husband, and never stopped till she came to the lower land.

After a while she reached a small house near a splendid castle. She went into the house and asked, could she stay there till morning. " You can," said the woman of the house, " and welcome."

Next day the woman of the house was washing clothes, for that was how she made a living. The princess fell to and helped her with the work. In the course of that day the Queen of Tir na n-Og and the husband of the princess were married.

Near the castle, and not far from the washer-woman's, lived a henwife with two ragged little daughters. One of them came around the washer-woman's house to play. The child looked so poor and her clothes were so torn and dirty that the princess took pity on her, and cut the clothes with the scissors which she had.

That moment the most beautiful dress of cloth of gold ever seen on woman or child in that king-dom was on the henwife's daughter.

When she saw what she had on, the child ran home to her mother as fast as ever she could go.

"Who gave you that dress?" asked the hen-wife.

"A strange woman that is in that house be-yond," said the little girl, pointing to the washer-woman's house.

The henwife went straight to the Queen of Tir na n-Og and said: "There is a strange woman in the place, who will be likely to take your husband from you, unless you banish her away or do some-thing to her; for she has a pair of scissors differ-ent from anything ever seen or heard of in this country."

When the queen heard this she sent word to the princess that, unless the scissors were given up to her without delay, she would have the head off her.

The princess said she would give up the scissors if the queen would let her pass one night with her husband.

The queen answered that she was willing to give her the one night. The princess came and gave up the scissors, and went to her own husband; but the queen had given him a drink, and he fell asleep, and never woke till after the princess had gone in the morning.

Next day another daughter of the henwife went to the washerwoman's house to play. She was wretched-looking, her head being covered with scabs and sores.

The princess drew the comb three times over the child's head, cured it, and covered it with beautiful golden hair. The little girl ran home and told her mother how the strange woman had drawn the comb over her head, cured it, and given her beautiful golden hair.

The henwife hurried off to the queen and said: "That strange woman has a comb with wonderful power to cure, and give golden hair; and she'll take your husband from you unless you banish her or take her life."

The queen sent word to the princess that unless she gave up the comb, she would have her life.

The princess returned as answer that she would give up the comb if she might pass one night with the queen's husband.

The queen was willing, and gave her husband a draught as before. When the princess came, he was fast asleep, and did not waken till after she had gone in the morning.

On the third day the washerwoman and the princess went out to walk, and the first daughter of the henwife with them. When they were outside the town, the princess put the whistle to her mouth and blew. That moment the birds of the air flew to her from every direction in flocks. Among them was a bird of song and new tales.

The princess went to one side with the bird. "What means can I take," asked she, "against the queen to get back my husband? Is it best to kill her, and can I do it?"

"It is very hard," said the bird, "to kill her. There is no one in all Tir na n-Og who is able to take her life but her own husband. Inside a holly-tree in front of the castle is a wether, in the wether a duck, in the duck an egg, and in that egg is her heart and life. No man in Tir na n-Og can cut that holly-tree but her husband."

The princess blew the whistle again. A fox and a hawk came to her. She caught and put them into two boxes, which the washerwoman had with her, and took them to her new home.

When the henwife's daughter went home, she told her mother about the whistle. Away ran the henwife to the queen, and said: "That strange woman has a whistle that brings together all the birds of the air, and she'll have your husband yet, unless you take her head."

"I'll take the whistle from her, anyhow," said the queen. So she sent for the whistle.

The princess gave answer that she would give up the whistle if she might pass one night with the queen's husband.

The queen agreed, and gave him a draught as on the other nights. He was asleep when the princess came and when she went away.

Before going, the princess left a letter with his servant for the queen's husband, in which she told how she had followed him to Tir na n-Og, and had given the scissors, the comb, and the whistle, to pass three nights in his company, but had not spoken to him because the queen had given him sleeping draughts; that the life of the queen was in an egg, the egg in a duck, the duck in a wether, the wether in a holly-tree in front of the castle, and that no man could split the tree but himself.

As soon as he got the letter the husband took an axe, and went to the holly-tree. When he came to the tree he found the princess there before him, having the two boxes with the fox and the hawk in them.

He struck the tree a few blows; it split open, and out sprang the wether. He ran scarce twenty perches before the fox caught him. The fox tore him open; then the duck flew out. The duck had not flown fifteen perches when the hawk caught and killed her, smashing the egg. That instant the Queen of Tir na n-Og died.

The husband kissed and embraced his faithful wife. He gave a great feast; and when the feast was over, he burned the henwife with her house, built a palace for the washerwoman, and made his servant secretary.

They never left Tir na n-Og, and are living there happily now; and so may we live here.

THE WEAVER'S SON AND THE GIANT
OF THE WHITE HILL.

THERE was once a weaver in Erin who lived at the edge of a wood; and on a time when he had nothing to burn, he went out with his daughter to get fagots for the fire.

They gathered two bundles, and were ready to carry them home, when who should come along but a splendid-looking stranger on horseback. And he said to the weaver: "My good man, will you give me that girl of yours?"

"Indeed then I will not," said the weaver.

"I'll give you her weight in gold," said the stranger, and he put out the gold there on the ground.

So the weaver went home with the gold and without the daughter. He buried the gold in the garden, without letting his wife know what he had done. When she asked, "Where is our daughter?" the weaver said: "I sent her on an errand to a neighbor's house for things that I want."

Night came, but no sight of the girl. The next time he went for fagots, the weaver took his second daughter to the wood; and when they had two bundles gathered, and were ready to go home, a second stranger came on horseback, much finer than the first, and asked the weaver would he give him his daughter.

"I will not," said the weaver.

"Well," said the stranger, "I'll give you her

weight in silver if you 'll let her go with me; " and
he put the silver down before him.

The weaver carried home the silver and buried
it in the garden with the gold, and the daughter
went away with the man on horseback.

When he went again to the wood, the weaver took
his third daughter with him; and when they were
ready to go home, a third man came on horseback,
gave the weight of the third daughter in copper,
and took her away. The weaver buried the copper
with the gold and silver.

Now, the wife was lamenting and moaning night
and day for her three daughters, and gave the
weaver no rest till he told the whole story.

Now, a son was born to them; and when the boy
grew up and was going to school, he heard how his
three sisters had been carried away for their weight
in gold and silver and copper; and every day when
he came home he saw how his mother was lamenting and wandering outside in grief through the
fields and pits and ditches, so he asked her what
trouble was on her; but she would n't tell him
a word.

At last he came home crying from school one
day, and said: " I 'll not sleep three nights in one
house till I find my three sisters." Then he said to
his mother: " Make me three loaves of bread,
mother, for I am going on a journey."

Next day he asked had she the bread ready. She
said she had, and she was crying bitterly all the
time. " I 'm going to leave you now, mother,"
said he; " and I 'll come back when I have found
my three sisters."

He went away, and walked on till he was tired
and hungry; and then he sat down to eat the bread
that his mother had given him, when a red-haired

man came up and asked him for something to eat. "Sit down here," said the boy. He sat down, and the two ate till there was not a crumb of the bread left.

The boy told of the journey he was on; then the red-haired man said: "There may not be much use in your going, but here are three things that'll serve you, — the sword of sharpness, the cloth of plenty, and the cloak of darkness. No man can kill you while that sword is in your hand; and whenever you are hungry or dry, all you have to do is to spread the cloth and ask for what you'd like to eat or drink, and it will be there before you. When you put on the cloak, there won't be a man or a woman or a living thing in the world that'll see you, and you'll go to whatever place you have set your mind on quicker than any wind."

The red-haired man went his way, and the boy travelled on. Before evening a great shower came, and he ran for shelter to a large oak-tree. When he got near the tree his foot slipped, the ground opened, and down he went through the earth till he came to another country. When he was in the other country he put on the cloak of darkness and went ahead like a blast of wind, and never stopped till he saw a castle in the distance; and soon he was there. But he found nine gates closed before him, and no way to go through. It was written inside the cloak of darkness that his eldest sister lived in that castle.

He was not long at the gate looking in when a girl came to him and said, "Go on out of that; if you don't, you'll be killed."

"Do you go in," said he to the girl, "and tell my sister, the woman of this castle, to come out to me."

The girl ran in; out came the sister, and asked: "Why are you here, and what did you come for?"

"I have come to this country to find my three sisters, who were given away by my father for their weight in gold, silver, and copper; and you are my eldest sister."

She knew from what he said that he was her brother, so she opened the gates and brought him in, saying: "Don't wonder at anything you see in this castle. My husband is enchanted. I see him only at night. He goes off every morning, stays away all day, and comes home in the evening."

The sun went down; and while they were talking, the husband rushed in, and the noise of him was terrible. He came in the form of a ram, ran up stairs, and soon after came down a man.

"Who is this that's with you?" asked he of the wife.

"Oh! that's my brother, who has come from Erin to see me," said she.

Next morning, when the man of the castle was going off in the form of a ram, he turned to the boy and asked, "Will you stay a few days in my castle? You are welcome."

"Nothing would please me better," said the boy; "but I have made a vow never to sleep three nights in one house till I have found my three sisters."

"Well," said the ram, "since you must go, here is something for you." And pulling out a bit of his own wool, he gave it to the boy, saying: "Keep this; and whenever a trouble is on you, take it out, and call on what rams are in the world to help you."

Away went the ram.   The boy took farewell of
his sister, put on the cloak of darkness, and disappeared.   He travelled till hungry and tired, then
he sat down, took off the cloak of darkness, spread
the cloth of plenty, and asked for meat and drink.
After he had eaten and drunk his fill, he took up
the cloth, put on the cloak of darkness, and went
ahead, passing every wind that was before him, and
leaving every wind that was behind.

About an hour before sunset he saw the castle
in which his second sister lived.   When he reached
the gate, a girl came out to him and said: " Go
away from that gate, or you 'll be killed."

" I 'll not leave this till my sister who lives in
the castle comes out and speaks to me."

The girl ran in, and out came the sister.   When
she heard his story and his father's name, she knew
that he was her brother, and said: " Come into the
castle, but think nothing of what you 'll see or
hear.   I don't see my husband from morning till
night.   He goes and comes in a strange form, but
he is a man at night."

About sunset there was a terrible noise, and in
rushed the man of the castle in the form of a tre-
mendous salmon.   He went flapping upstairs;
but he was n't long there till he came down a fine-
looking man.

" Who is that with you? " asked he of the wife.
" I thought you would let no one into the castle
while I was gone."

" Oh! this is my brother, who has come to see
me," said she.

" If he 's your brother, he 's welcome," said the
man.

They supped, and then slept till morning.
When the man of the castle was going out again, in

" And is there no way to kill him? " asked the boy.

" I think not," said she.

" Well, if you'll give me something to eat, I'll stay here; and when the giant comes in, I'll do my best to kill him. But don't let on that I am here."

Then he put on the cloak of darkness, and no one could see him. When the giant came in, he had the bodies of two men on his back. He threw down the bodies and told the young woman to get them ready for his dinner. Then he snuffed around, and said: " There's some one here; I smell the blood of an Erineach."

" I don't think you do," said the young woman; " I can't see any one."

" Neither can I," said the giant; " but I smell a man."

With that the boy drew his sword; and when the giant was struck, he ran in the direction of the blow to give one back; then he was struck on the other side.

They were at one another this way, the giant and the boy with the cloak of darkness on him, till the giant had fifty wounds, and was covered with blood. Every minute he was getting a slash of a sword, but never could give one back. At last he called out: " Whoever you are, wait till to-morrow, and I'll face you then."

So the fighting stopped; and the young woman began to cry and lament as if her heart would break when she saw the state the giant was in. " Oh! you'll be with me no longer; you'll be killed now: what can I do alone without you?" and she tried to please him, and washed his wounds.

" Don't be afraid," said the giant; " this one, whoever he is, will not kill me, for there is no man in the world that can kill me." Then the giant went to bed, and was well in the morning.

Next day the giant and the boy began in the middle of the forenoon, and fought till the middle of the afternoon. The giant was covered with wounds, and he had not given one blow to the boy, and could not see him, for he was always in his cloak of darkness. So the giant had to ask for rest till next morning.

While the young woman was washing and dressing the wounds of the giant she cried and lamented all the time, saying: "What 'll become of me now? I 'm afraid you 'll be killed this time; and how can I live here without you?"

"Have no fear for me," said the giant; "I 'll put your mind at rest. In the bottom of the sea is a chest locked and bound, in that chest is a duck, in the duck an egg; and I never can be killed unless some one gets the egg from the duck in the chest at the bottom of the sea, and rubs it on the mole that is under my right breast."

While the giant was telling this to the woman to put her mind at rest, who should be listening to the story but the boy in the cloak of darkness. The minute he heard of the chest in the sea, he thought of the salmons. So off he hurried to the seashore, which was not far away. Then he took out the fin that his eldest sister's husband had given him, and called on what salmons were in the sea to bring up the chest with the duck inside, and put it out on the beach before him.

He had not long to wait till he saw nothing but salmon, — the whole sea was covered with them, moving to land; and they put the chest out on the beach before him.

But the chest was locked and strong; how could

he open it? He thought of the rams; and taking out the lock of wool, said: " I want what rams are in the world to come and break open this chest! "

That minute the rams of the world were running to the seashore, each with a terrible pair of horns on him; and soon they battered the chest to splinters. Out flew the duck, and away she went over the sea.

The boy took out the feather, and said: " I want what eagles are in the world to get me the egg from that duck."

That minute the duck was surrounded by the eagles of the world, and the egg was soon brought to the boy. He put the feather, the wool, and the fin in his pocket, put on the cloak of darkness, and went to the castle on the white hill, and told the young woman, when she was dressing the wounds of the giant again, to raise up his arm.

Next day they fought till the middle of the afternoon. The giant was almost cut to pieces, and called for a cessation.

The young woman hurried to dress the wounds, and he said: " I see you would help me if you could: you are not able. But never fear, I shall not be killed." Then she raised his arm to wash away the blood, and the boy, who was there in his cloak of darkness, struck the mole with the egg. The giant died that minute.

The boy took the young woman to the castle of his third sister. Next day he went back for the treasures of the giant, and there was more gold in the castle than one horse could draw.

They spent nine days in the castle of the eagle with the third sister. Then the boy gave back the feather, and the two went on till they came to the castle of the salmon, where they spent nine more days with the second sister; and he gave back the fin.

When they came to the castle of the ram, they spent fifteen days with the first sister, and had great feasting and enjoyment. Then the boy gave back the lock of wool to the ram, and taking farewell of his sister and her husband, set out for home with the young woman of the white castle, who was now his wife, bringing presents from the three daughters to their father and mother.

At last they reached the opening near the tree, came up through the ground, and went on to where he met the red-haired man. Then he spread the cloth of plenty, asked for every good meat and drink, and called the red-haired man. He came. The three sat down, ate and drank with enjoyment.

When they had finished, the boy gave back to the red-haired man the cloak of darkness, the sword of sharpness, and the cloth of plenty, and thanked him.

"You were kind to me," said the red-haired man; "you gave me of your bread when I asked for it, and told me where you were going. I took pity on you; for I knew you never could get what you wanted unless I helped you. I am the brother of the eagle, the salmon, and the ram."

They parted. The boy went home, built a castle with the treasure of the giant, and lived happily with his parents and wife.

FAIR, BROWN, AND TREMBLING.

KING AEDH CÚRUCHA lived in Tir Conal, and he had three daughters, whose names were Fair, Brown, and Trembling.

Fair and Brown had new dresses, and went to church every Sunday. Trembling was kept at home to do the cooking and work. They would not let her go out of the house at all; for she was more beautiful than the other two, and they were in dread she might marry before themselves.

They carried on in this way for seven years. At the end of seven years the son of the king of Omanya[1] fell in love with the eldest sister.

One Sunday morning, after the other two had gone to church, the old henwife came into the kitchen to Trembling, and said: "It's at church you ought to be this day, instead of working here at home."

"How could I go?" said Trembling. "I have no clothes good enough to wear at church; and if my sisters were to see me there, they'd kill me for going out of the house."

"I'll give you," said the henwife, "a finer dress than either of them has ever seen. And now tell me what dress will you have?"

"I'll have," said Trembling, "a dress as white as snow, and green shoes for my feet."

Then the henwife put on the cloak of darkness,

---

[1] The ancient Emania in Ulster.

clipped a piece from the old clothes the young woman had on, and asked for the whitest robes in the world and the most beautiful that could be found, and a pair of green shoes.

That moment she had the robe and the shoes, and she brought them to Trembling, who put them on. When Trembling was dressed and ready, the henwife said: " I have a honey-bird here to sit on your right shoulder, and a honey-finger to put on your left. At the door stands a milk-white mare, with a golden saddle for you to sit on, and a golden bridle to hold in your hand."

Trembling sat on the golden saddle ; and when she was ready to start, the henwife said: " You must not go inside the door of the church, and the minute the people rise up at the end of Mass, do you make off, and ride home as fast as the mare will carry you."

When Trembling came to the door of the church there was no one inside who could get a glimpse of her but was striving to know who she was; and when they saw her hurrying away at the end of Mass, they ran out to overtake her. But no use in their running; she was away before any man could come near her. From the minute she left the church till she got home, she overtook the wind before her, and outstripped the wind behind.

She came down at the door, went in, and found the henwife had dinner ready. She put off the white robes, and had on her old dress in a twinkling.

When the two sisters came home the henwife asked: " Have you any news to-day from the church? "

" We have great news," said they. " We saw a wonderful, grand lady at the church-door. The like of the robes she had we have never seen on woman before.   It's little that was thought of our dresses beside what she had on; and there was n't a man at the church, from the king to the beggar, but was trying to look at her and know who she was."

The sisters would give no peace till they had two dresses like the robes of the strange lady; but honey-birds and honey-fingers were not to be found.

Next Sunday the two sisters went to church again, and left the youngest at home to cook the dinner.

After they had gone, the henwife came in and asked: " Will you go to church to-day? "

" I would go," said Trembling, " if I could get the going."

" What robe will you wear? " asked the henwife.

" The finest black satin that can be found, and red shoes for my feet."

" What color do you want the mare to be? "

" I want her to be so black and so glossy that I can see myself in her body."

The henwife put on the cloak of darkness, and asked for the robes and the mare.   That moment she had them.   When Trembling was dressed, the henwife put the honey-bird on her right shoulder and the honey-finger on her left.   The saddle on the mare was silver, and so was the bridle.

When Trembling sat in the saddle and was going away, the henwife ordered her strictly not to go inside the door of the church, but to rush away as soon as the people rose at the end of Mass, and hurry home on the mare before any man could stop her.

That Sunday the people were more astonished

than ever, and gazed at her more than the first
time; and all they were thinking of was to know
who she was. But they had no chance; for the moment the people rose at the end of Mass she slipped
from the church, was in the silver saddle, and home
before a man could stop her or talk to her.

The henwife had the dinner ready. Trembling
took off her satin robe, and had on her old clothes
before her sisters got home.

"What news have you to-day?" asked the
henwife of the sisters when they came from the
church.

"Oh, we saw the grand strange lady again!
And it's little that any man could think of our
dresses after looking at the robes of satin that she
had on! And all at church, from high to low,
had their mouths open, gazing at her, and no man
was looking at us."

The two sisters gave neither rest nor peace
till they got dresses as nearly like the strange
lady's robes as they could find. Of course they
were not so good; for the like of those robes
could not be found in Erin.

When the third Sunday came, Fair and Brown
went to church dressed in black satin. They left
Trembling at home to work in the kitchen, and
told her to be sure and have dinner ready when
they came back.

After they had gone and were out of sight, the
henwife came to the kitchen and said: "Well, my
dear, are you for church to-day?"

"I would go if I had a new dress to wear."

"I'll get you any dress you ask for. What
dress would you like?" asked the henwife.

"A dress red as a rose from the waist down, and
white as snow from the waist up; a cape of green

on my shoulders; and a hat on my head with a red, a white, and a green feather in it; and shoes for my feet with the toes red, the middle white, and the backs and heels green."

The henwife put on the cloak of darkness, wished for all these things, and had them. When Trembling was dressed, the henwife put the honey-bird on her right shoulder and the honey-finger on her left, and placing the hat on her head, clipped a few hairs from one lock and a few from another with her scissors, and that moment the most beautiful golden hair was flowing down over the girl's shoulders. Then the henwife asked what kind of a mare she would ride. She said white, with blue and gold-colored diamond-shaped spots all over her body, on her back a saddle of gold, and on her head a golden bridle.

The mare stood there before the door, and a bird sitting between her ears, which began to sing as soon as Trembling was in the saddle, and never stopped till she came home from the church.

The fame of the beautiful strange lady had gone out through the world, and all the princes and great men that were in it came to church that Sunday, each one hoping that it was himself would have her home with him after Mass.

The son of the king of Omanya forgot all about the eldest sister, and remained outside the church, so as to catch the strange lady before she could hurry away.

The church was more crowded than ever before, and there were three times as many outside. There was such a throng before the church that Trembling could only come inside the gate.

As soon as the people were rising at the end of Mass, the lady slipped out through the gate, was in the golden saddle in an instant, and sweeping away ahead of the wind. But if she was, the prince of Omanya was at her side, and, seizing her by the foot, he ran with the mare for thirty perches, and never let go of the beautiful lady till the shoe was pulled from her foot, and he was left behind with it in his hand. She came home as fast as the mare could carry her, and was thinking all the time that the henwife would kill her for losing the shoe.

Seeing her so vexed and so changed in the face, the old woman asked: "What's the trouble that's on you now?"

"Oh! I've lost one of the shoes off my feet," said Trembling.

"Don't mind that; don't be vexed," said the henwife; "maybe it's the best thing that ever happened to you."

Then Trembling gave up all the things she had to the henwife, put on her old clothes, and went to work in the kitchen. When the sisters came home, the henwife asked: "Have you any news from the church?"

"We have indeed," said they; "for we saw the grandest sight to-day. The strange lady came again, in grander array than before. On herself and the horse she rode were the finest colors of the world, and between the ears of the horse was a bird which never stopped singing from the time she came till she went away. The lady herself is the most beautiful woman ever seen by man in Erin."

After Trembling had disappeared from the church, the son of the king of Omanya said to the other kings' sons: "I will have that lady for my own."

They all said: "You didn't win her just by taking

the shoe off her foot, you 'll have to win her by the point of the sword; you 'll have to fight for her with us before you can call her your own."

"Well," said the son of the king of Omanya, "when I find the lady that shoe will fit, I 'll fight for her, never fear, before I leave her to any of you."

Then all the kings' sons were uneasy, and anxious to know who was she that lost the shoe; and they began to travel all over Erin to know could they find her. The prince of Omanya and all the others went in a great company together, and made the round of Erin; they went everywhere, — north, south, east, and west. They visited every place where a woman was to be found, and left not a house in the kingdom they did not search, to know could they find the woman the shoe would fit, not caring whether she was rich or poor, of high or low degree.

The prince of Omanya always kept the shoe; and when the young women saw it, they had great hopes, for it was of proper size, neither large nor small, and it would beat any man to know of what material it was made. One thought it would fit her if she cut a little from her great toe; and another, with too short a foot, put something in the tip of her stocking. But no use, they only spoiled their feet, and were curing them for months afterwards.

The two sisters, Fair and Brown, heard that the princes of the world were looking all over Erin for the woman that could wear the shoe, and every day they were talking of trying it on; and one day Trembling spoke up and said: "Maybe it 's my foot that the shoe will fit."

"Oh, the breaking of the dog's foot on you! Why say so when you were at home every Sunday?"

They were that way waiting, and scolding the younger sister, till the princes were near the place. The day they were to come, the sisters put Trembling in a closet, and locked the door on her. When the company came to the house, the prince of Omanya gave the shoe to the sisters. But though they tried and tried, it would fit neither of them.

" Is there any other young woman in the house?" asked the prince.

" There is," said Trembling, speaking up in the closet; " I'm here."

" Oh! we have her for nothing but to put out the ashes," said the sisters.

But the prince and the others would n't leave the house till they had seen her; so the two sisters had to open the door. When Trembling came out, the shoe was given to her, and it fitted exactly.

The prince of Omanya looked at her and said: " You are the woman the shoe fits, and you are the woman I took the shoe from."

Then Trembling spoke up, and said: " Do you stay here till I return."

Then she went to the henwife's house. The old woman put on the cloak of darkness, got everything for her she had the first Sunday at church, and put her on the white mare in the same fashion. Then Trembling rode along the highway to the front of the house. All who saw her the first time said: " This is the lady we saw at church."

Then she went away a second time, and a second time came back on the black mare in the second dress which the henwife gave her. All who saw her the second Sunday said: " That is the lady we saw at church."

A third time she asked for a short absence, and soon came back on the third mare and in the third dress. All who saw her the third time said: " That is the lady we saw at church." Every man was satisfied, and knew that she was the woman.

Then all the princes and great men spoke up, and said to the son of the king of Omanya: " You 'll have to fight now for her before we let her go with you."

" I 'm here before you, ready for combat," answered the prince.

Then the son of the king of Lochlin stepped forth. The struggle began, and a terrible struggle it was. They fought for nine hours; and then the son of the king of Lochlin stopped, gave up his claim, and left the field. Next day the son of the king of Spain fought six hours, and yielded his claim. On the third day the son of the king of Nyerfói fought eight hours, and stopped. The fourth day the son of the king of Greece fought six hours, and stopped. On the fifth day no more strange princes wanted to fight; and all the sons of kings in Erin said they would not fight with a man of their own land, that the strangers had had their chance, and as no others came to claim the woman, she belonged of right to the son of the king of Omanya.

The marriage-day was fixed, and the invitations were sent out. The wedding lasted for a year and a day. When the wedding was over, the king's son brought home the bride, and when the time came a son was born. The young woman sent for her eldest sister, Fair, to be with her and care for her. One day, when Trembling was well, and when her husband was away hunting, the two sisters went out to walk; and when they came to the seaside, the eldest pushed the youngest sister in. A great whale came and swallowed her.

The eldest sister came home alone, and the husband asked, "Where is your sister?"

" She has gone home to her father in Ballyshannon; now that I am well, I don't need her."

"Well," said the husband, looking at her, " I 'm in dread it 's my wife that has gone."

" Oh! no," said she; " it 's my sister Fair that 's gone."

Since the sisters were very much alike, the prince was in doubt. That night he put his sword between them, and said: " If you are my wife, this sword will get warm; if not, it will stay cold."

In the morning when he rose up, the sword was as cold as when he put it there.

It happened when the two sisters were walking by the seashore, that a little cowboy was down by the water minding cattle, and saw Fair push Trembling into the sea; and next day, when the tide came in, he saw the whale swim up and throw her out on the sand. When she was on the sand she said to the cowboy: " When you go home in the evening with the cows, tell the master that my sister Fair pushed me into the sea yesterday; that a whale swallowed me, and then threw me out, but will come again and swallow me with the coming of the next tide; then he 'll go out with the tide, and come again with to-morrow's tide, and throw me again on the strand. The whale will cast me out three times. I 'm under the enchantment of this whale, and cannot leave the beach or escape myself. Unless my husband saves me before I 'm swallowed the fourth

time, I shall be lost. He must come and shoot
the whale with a silver bullet when he turns on the
broad of his back. Under the breast-fin of the
whale is a reddish-brown spot. My husband must
hit him in that spot, for it is the only place in
which he can be killed."

When the cowboy got home, the eldest sister
gave him a draught of oblivion, and he did not tell.

Next day he went again to the sea. The whale
came and cast Trembling on shore again. She
asked the boy: " Did you tell the master what I
told you to tell him?"

" I did not," said he; " I forgot."

" How did you forget?" asked she.

" The woman of the house gave me a drink that
made me forget."

" Well, don't forget telling him this night; and
if she gives you a drink, don't take it from her."

As soon as the cowboy came home, the eldest
sister offered him a drink. He refused to take it
till he had delivered his message and told all to the
master. The third day the prince went down with
his gun and a silver bullet in it. He was not long
down when the whale came and threw Trembling
upon the beach as the two days before. She had
no power to speak to her husband till he had
killed the whale. Then the whale went out, turned
over once on the broad of his back, and showed
the spot for a moment only. That moment the
prince fired. He had but the one chance, and
a short one at that; but he took it, and hit the
spot, and the whale, mad with pain, made the sea
all around red with blood, and died.

That minute Trembling was able to speak, and
went home with her husband, who sent word to
her father what the eldest sister had done. The

father came, and told him any death he chose to give her to give it. The prince told the father he would leave her life and death with himself. The father had her put out then on the sea in a barrel, with provisions in it for seven years.

In time Trembling had a second child, a daughter. The prince and she sent the cowboy to school, and trained him up as one of their own children, and said: "If the little girl that is born to us now lives, no other man in the world will get her but him."

The cowboy and the prince's daughter lived on till they were married. The mother said to her husband: "You could not have saved me from the whale but for the little cowboy; on that account I don't grudge him my daughter."

The son of the king of Omanya and Trembling had fourteen children, and they lived happily till the two died of old age.

THE KING OF ERIN AND THE QUEEN OF THE LONESOME ISLAND.

THERE was a king in Erin long ago, and this king went out hunting one day, but saw nothing till near sunset, when what should come across him but a black pig.

"Since I 've seen nothing all day but this black pig, I 'll be at her now," said the king; so he put spurs to his horse and raced after the pig.

When the pig was on a hill he was in the valley behind her; when he was on a hill, the pig was in the valley before him. At last they came to the sea-side, and the pig rushed out into the deep water straight from the shore. The king spurred on his horse and followed the black pig through the sea till his horse failed under him and was drowned.

Then the king swam on himself till he was growing weak, and said: "It was for the death of me that the black pig came in my way."

But he swam on some distance yet, till at last he saw land. The pig went up on an island; the king too went on shore, and said to himself: "Oh! it is for no good that I came here; there is neither house nor shelter to be seen." But he cheered up after a while, walked around, and said: "I 'm a useless man if I can't find shelter in some place."

After going on a short space he saw a great castle in a valley before him. When he came to the front of the castle he saw that it had a low door

with a broad threshold all covered with sharp-edged
razors, and a low lintel of long-pointed needles.
The path to the castle was covered with gravel of
gold.   The king came up, and went in with a jump
over the razors and under the needles.   When inside he saw a great fire on a broad hearth, and
said to himself, " I 'll sit down here, dry **my**
clothes, and warm my body at this fire."

As he sat and warmed himself, a table came out
before him with every sort of food and drink, without his seeing any one bring it.

" Upon my honor and power," said the king of
Erin, "there is nothing bad in this!   I 'll eat and
drink my fill."

Then he fell to, and ate and drank his fill.
When he had grown tired, he looked behind him,
and if he did he saw a fine room, and in it a bed
covered with gold.   " Well," said he, " I 'll go
back and sleep in that bed a while, I 'm so tired."

He stretched himself on the bed and fell asleep.
In the night he woke up, and felt the presence **of a**
woman in the room.   He reached out his hand
towards her and spoke, but got no answer; she
was silent.

When morning came, and he made his way **out**
of the castle, she spread a beautiful garden with
her Druidic spells over the island, — so great **that**
though he travelled through it all day he could **not**
escape from it.   At sunset he was back at the door
of the castle; and in he went over the razors and
under the needles, sat at the fire, and the table came
out before him as on the previous evening.   He ate,
drank, and slept on the bed; and when he woke
in the night, there was the woman in the room;
but she was silent and unseen as before.

When he went out on the second morning the

king of Erin saw a garden three times more beautiful than the one of the day before. He travelled
all day, but could not escape, — could not get out
of the garden. At sunset he was back at the door
of the castle; in he went over the razors and under
the needles, ate, drank, and slept, as before.

In the middle of the night he woke up, and felt the
presence of the woman in the room. "Well," said
he, "it is a wonderful thing for me to pass three
nights in a room with a woman, and not see her
nor know who she is!"

"You won't have that to say again, king of
Erin," answered a voice. And that moment the
room was filled with a bright light, and the king
looked upon the finest woman he had ever seen.
"Well, king of Erin, you are on Lonesome Island.
I am the black pig that enticed you over the land
and through the sea to this place, and I am queen
of Lonesome Island. My two sisters and I are under a Druidic spell, and we cannot escape from this
spell till your son and mine shall free us. Now,
king of Erin, I will give you a boat to-morrow morning, and do you sail away to your own kingdom."

In the morning she went with him to the seashore to the boat. The king gave the prow of the
boat to the sea, and its stern to the land; then he
raised the sails, and went his way. The music he
had was the roaring of the wind with the whistling
of eels, and he broke neither oar nor mast till he
landed under his own castle in Erin.

Three quarters of a year after, the queen of
Lonesome Island gave birth to a son. She reared
him with care from day to day and year to year
till he was a splendid youth. She taught him
the learning of wise men one half of the day, and
warlike exercises with Druidic spells the other half.

One time the young man, the prince of Lonesome Island, came in from hunting, and found his mother sobbing and crying.

" Oh ! what has happened to you, mother? " he asked.

" My son, great grief has come on me. A friend of mine is going to be killed to-morrow."

" Who is he? "

" The king of Erin. The king of Spain has come against him with a great army. He wishes to sweep him and his men from the face of the earth, and take the kingdom himself."

" Well, what can we do? If I were there, I 'd help the king of Erin."

" Since you say that, my son, I 'll send you this very evening. With the power of my Druidic spells, you 'll be in Erin in the morning."

The prince of Lonesome Island went away that night, and next morning at the rising of the sun he drew up his boat under the king's castle in Erin. He went ashore, and saw the whole land black with the forces of the king of Spain, who was getting ready to attack the king of Erin and sweep him and his men from the face of the earth.

The prince went straight to the king of Spain, and said, " I ask one day's truce."

" You shall have it, my champion," answered the king of Spain.

The prince then went to the castle of the king of Erin, and stayed there that day as a guest. Next morning early he dressed himself in his champion's array, and, taking his nine-edged sword, he went down alone to the king of Spain, and, standing before him, bade him guard himself.

They closed in conflict, the king of Spain with

all his forces on one side, and the prince of
Lonesome Island on the other. They fought an
awful battle that day from sunrise till sunset.
They made soft places hard, and hard places soft;
they made high places low, and low places high;
they brought water out of the centre of hard gray
rocks, and made dry rushes soft in the most distant parts of Erin till sunset; and when the sun
went down, the king of Spain and his last man
were dead on the field.

Neither the king of Erin nor his forces took part
in the battle. They had no need, and they had
no chance.

Now the king of Erin had two sons, who were
such cowards that they hid themselves from fright
during the battle; but their mother told the king
of Erin that her elder son was the man who had
destroyed the king of Spain and all his men.

There was great rejoicing and a feast at the
castle of the king of Erin. At the end of the feast
the queen said: " I wish to give the last cup to
this stranger who is here as a guest; " and taking
him to an adjoining chamber which had a window
right over the sea, she seated him in the open window and gave him a cup of drowsiness to drink.
When he had emptied the cup and closed his eyes,
she pushed him out into the darkness.

The prince of Lonesome Island swam on the
water for four days and nights, till he came to a
rock in the ocean, and there he lived for three
months, eating the seaweeds of the rock, till one
foggy day a vessel came near and the captain cried
out: " We shall be wrecked on this rock! " Then
he said, " There is some one on the rock; go and
see who it is."

They landed, and found the prince, his clothes all

gone, his body black from the seaweed, which was growing all over it.

" Who are you? " asked the captain.

" Give me first to eat and drink, and then I 'll talk," said he.

They brought him food and drink; and when he had eaten and drunk, the prince said to the captain: " What part of the world have you come from? "

" I have just sailed from Lonesome Island," said the captain. " I was obliged to sail away, for fire was coming from every side to burn my ship."

" Would you like to go back? "

" I should indeed."

" Well, turn around; you 'll have no trouble if I am with you."

The captain returned. The queen of Lonesome Island was standing on the shore as the ship came in.

" Oh, my child! " cried she, " why have you been away so long? "

" The queen of Erin threw me into the sea after I had kept the head of the king of Erin on him, and saved her life too."

" Well, my son, that will come up against the queen of Erin on another day."

Now, the prince lived on Lonesome Island three years longer, till one time he came home from hunting, and found his mother wringing her hands and shedding bitter tears.

" Oh! what has happened? " asked he.

" I am weeping because the king of Spain has gone to take vengeance on the king of Erin for the death of his father, whom you killed."

" Well, mother, I 'll go to help the king of Erin, if you give me leave."

" Since you have said it, you shall go this very night."

He went to the shore. Putting the prow of his bark to the sea and her stern to land, he raised high the sails, and heard no sound as he went but the pleasant wind and the whistling of eels, till he pulled up his boat next morning under the castle of the king of Erin and went on shore.

The whole country was black with the troops of the king of Spain, who was just ready to attack, when the prince stood before him, and asked a truce till next morning.

" That you shall have, my champion," answered the king. So there was peace for that day.

Next morning at sunrise, the prince faced the king of Spain and his army, and there followed a struggle more terrible than that with his father; but at sunset neither the king of Spain nor one of his men was left alive.

The two sons of the king of Erin were frightened almost to death, and hid during the battle, so that no one saw them or knew where they were. But when the king of Spain and his army were destroyed, the queen said to the king: " My elder son has saved us." Then she went to bed, and taking the blood of a chicken in her mouth, spat it out, saying: " This is my heart's blood; and nothing can cure me now but three bottles of water from Tubber Tintye, the flaming well."

When the prince was told of the sickness of the queen of Erin, he came to her and said: " I 'll go for the water if your two sons will go with me."

" They shall go," said the queen; and away went the three young men towards the East, in search of the flaming well.

In the morning they came to a house on the

roadside; and going in, they saw a woman who had washed herself in a golden basin which stood before her. She was then wetting her head with the water in the basin, and combing her hair with a golden comb. She threw back her hair, and looking at the prince, said: " You are welcome, sister's son. What is on ycu? Is it the misfortune of the world that has brought you here? "

" It is not; I am going to Tubber Tintye for three bottles of water."

" That is what you 'll never do; no man can cross the fiery river or go through the enchantments around Tubber Tintye. Stay here with me, and I 'll give you all I have."

" No, I cannot stay, I must go on."

" Well, you 'll be in your other aunt's house to-morrow night, and she will tell you all."

Next morning, when they were getting ready to take the road, the elder son of the queen of Erin was frightened at what he had heard, and said: " I am sick; I cannot go farther."

" Stop here where you are till I come back," said the prince. Then he went on with the younger brother, till at sunset they came to a house where they saw a woman wetting her head from a golden basin, and combing her hair with a golden comb. She threw back her hair, looked at the prince, and said: " You are welcome, sister's son! What brought you to this place? Was it the misfortune of the world that brought you to live under Druidic spells like me and my sisters? " This was the elder sister of the queen of the Lonesome Island.

" No," said the prince; " I am going to Tubber Tintye for three bottles of water from the flaming well."

" Oh, sister's son, it 's a hard journey you 're on!

But stay here to-night; to-morrow morning I'll tell you all."

In the morning the prince's aunt said: "The queen of the Island of Tubber Tintye has an enormous castle, in which she lives. She has a countless army of giants, beasts, and monsters to guard the castle and the flaming well. There are thousands upon thousands of them, of every form and size. When they get drowsy, and sleep comes on them, they sleep for seven years without waking. The queen has twelve attendant maidens, who live in twelve chambers. She is in the thirteenth and innermost chamber herself. The queen and the maidens sleep during the same seven years as the giants and beasts. When the seven years are over, they all wake up, and none of them sleep again for seven other years. If any man could enter the castle during the seven years of sleep, he could do what he liked. But the island on which the castle stands is girt by a river of fire and surrounded by a belt of poison-trees."

The aunt now blew on a horn, and all the birds of the air gathered around her from every place under the heavens, and she asked each in turn where it dwelt, and each told her; but none knew of the flaming well, till an old eagle said: "I left Tubber Tintye to-day."

"How are all the people there?" asked the aunt.

"They are all asleep since yesterday morning," answered the old eagle.

The aunt dismissed the birds; and turning to the prince, said, "Here is a bridle for you. Go to the stables, shake the bridle, and put it on whatever horse runs out to meet you."

Now the second son of the queen of Erin said:

" I am too sick to go farther."

"Well, stay here till I come back," said the prince, who took the bridle and went out.

The prince of the Lonesome Island stood in front of his aunt's stables, shook the bridle, and out came a dirty, lean little shaggy horse.

" Sit on my back, son of the king of Erin and the queen of Lonesome Island," said the little shaggy horse.

This was the first the prince had heard of his father. He had often wondered who he might be, but had never heard who he was before.

He mounted the horse, which said: "Keep a firm grip now, for I shall clear the river of fire at a single bound, and pass the poison-trees; but if you touch any part of the trees, even with a thread of the clothing that's on you, you'll never eat another bite; and as I rush by the end of the castle of Tubber Tintye with the speed of the wind, you must spring from my back through an open window that is there; and if you don't get in at the window, you're done for. I'll wait for you outside till you are ready to go back to Erin."

The prince did as the little horse told him. They crossed the river of fire, escaped the touch of the poison-trees, and as the horse shot past the castle, the prince sprang through the open window, and came down safe and sound inside.

The whole place, enormous in extent, was filled with sleeping giants and monsters of sea and land, — great whales, long slippery eels, bears, and beasts of every form and kind. The prince passed through them and over them till he came to a great stairway. At the head of the stairway he went into a chamber, where he found the most beautiful woman he had ever seen, stretched on a

couch asleep. " I 'll have nothing to say to you,"
thought he, and went on to the next; and so he
looked into twelve chambers. In each was a
woman more beautiful than the one before. But
when he reached the thirteenth chamber and
opened the door, the flash of gold took the sight
from his eyes. He stood a while till the sight
came back, and then entered. In the great bright
chamber was a golden couch, resting on wheels of
gold. The wheels turned continually; the couch
went round and round, never stopping night or
day. On the couch lay the queen of Tubber
Tintye; and if her twelve maidens were beautiful,
they would not be beautiful if seen near her. At
the foot of the couch was Tubber Tintye itself, — the
well of fire. There was a golden cover upon the
well, and it went around continually with the couch
of the queen.

" Upon my word," said the prince, " I 'll rest
here a while." And he went up on the couch,
and never left it for six days and nights.

On the seventh morning he said, " It is time for
me now to leave this place." So he came down
and filled the three bottles with water from the
flaming well. In the golden chamber was a table
of gold, and on the table a leg of mutton with a
loaf of bread; and if all the men in Erin were to
eat for a twelvemonth from the table, the mutton
and the bread would be in the same form after the
eating as before.

The prince sat down, ate his fill of the loaf and
the leg of mutton, and left them as he had found
them. Then he rose up, took his three bottles,
put them in his wallet, and was leaving the
chamber, when he said to himself: " It would be a
shame to go away without leaving something by

which the queen may know who was here while she slept." So he wrote a letter, saying that the son of the king of Erin and the queen of the Lonesome Island had spent six days and nights in the golden chamber of Tubber Tintye, had taken away three bottles of water from the flaming well, and had eaten from the table of gold. Putting this letter under the pillow of the queen, he went out, stood in the open window, sprang on the back of the lean and shaggy little horse, and passed the trees and the river unharmed.

When they were near his aunt's house, the horse stopped, and said: "Put your hand into my ear, and draw out of it a Druidic rod; then cut me into four quarters, and strike each quarter with the rod. Each one of them will become the son of a king, for four princes were enchanted and turned into the lean little shaggy horse that carried you to Tubber Tintye. When you have freed the four princes from this form you can free your two aunts from the spell that is on them, and take them with you to Lonesome Island."

The prince did as the horse desired; and straightway four princes stood before him, and thanking him for what he had done, they departed at once, each to his own kingom.

The prince removed the spell from his aunts, and, travelling with them and the two sons of the queen of Erin, all soon appeared at the castle of the king.

When they were near the door of their mother's chamber, the elder of the two sons of the queen of Erin stepped up to the prince of Lonesome Island, snatched the three bottles from the wallet that he had at his side, and running up to his

mother's bed, said: " Here, mother, are the three
bottles of water which I brought you from Tubber
Tintye."

" Thank you, my son; you have saved my life,"
said she.

The prince went on his bark and sailed away
with his aunts to Lonesome Island, where he lived
with his mother seven years.

When seven years were over, the queen of
Tubber Tintye awoke from her sleep in the golden
chamber; and with her the twelve maidens and all
the giants, beasts, and monsters that slept in the
great castle.

When the queen opened her eyes, she saw a boy
about six years old playing by himself on the floor.
He was very beautiful and bright, and he had gold
on his forehead and silver on his poll. When she
saw the child, she began to cry and wring her
hands, and said: " Some man has been here while
I slept."

Straightway she sent for her Seandallglic (old
blind sage), told him about the child, and asked:
" What am I to do now? "

The old blind sage thought a while, and then
said: " Whoever was here must be a hero; for the
child has gold on his forehead and silver on his
poll, and he never went from this place without
leaving his name behind him. Let search be
made, and we shall know who he was."

Search was made, and at last they found the
letter of the prince under the pillow of the couch.
The queen was now glad, and proud of the child.

Next day she assembled all her forces, her
giants and guards; and when she had them drawn
up in line, the army was seven miles long from van
to rear. The queen opened through the river of

fire a safe way for the host, and led it on till she
came to the castle of the king of Erin.   She held
all the land near the castle, so the king had the sea
on one side, and the army of the queen of Tubber
Tintye on the other, ready to destroy him and all
that he had.   The queen sent a herald for the
king to come down.

"What are you going to do?" asked the king
when he came to her tent.   "I have had trouble
enough in my life already, without having more
of it now."

"Find for me," said the queen, "the man who
came to my castle and entered the golden chamber
of Tubber Tintye while I slept, or I'll sweep you
and all you have from the face of the earth."

The king of Erin called down his elder son, and
asked: "Did you enter the chamber of the queen
of Tubber Tintye?"

"I did."

"Go, then, and tell her so, and save us."

He went; and when he told the queen, she said:
"If you entered my chamber, then mount my gray
steed."

He mounted the steed; and if he did, the steed
rose in the air with a bound, hurled him off his
back, in a moment, threw him on a rock, and dashed
the brains out of his head.

The king called down his second son, who said
that he had been in the golden chamber.   Then he
mounted the gray steed, which killed him as it had
his brother.

Now the queen called the king again, and said:
"Unless you bring the man who entered my gold-
en chamber while I slept, I'll not leave a sign
of you or anything you have upon the face of
the earth."

Straightway the king sent a message to the queen of Lonesome Island, saying: " Come to me with your son and your two sisters ! "

The queen set out next morning, and at sunset she drew up her boat under the castle of the king of Erin. Glad were they to see her at the castle, for great dread was on all.

Next morning the king went down to the queen of Tubber Tintye, who said: " Bring me the man who entered my castle, or I 'll destroy you and all you have in Erin this day."

The king went up to the castle; immediately the prince of Lonesome Island went to the queen.

" Are you the man who entered my castle? " asked she.

" I don't know," said the prince.

" Go up now on my gray steed ! " said the queen.

He sat on the gray steed, which rose under him into the sky. The prince stood on the back of the horse, and cut three times with his sword as he went up under the sun. When he came to the earth again, the queen of Tubber Tintye ran over to him, put his head on her bosom, and said: " You are the man."

Now she called the queen of Erin to her tent, and drawing from her own pocket a belt of silk, slender as a cord, she said: " Put this on."

The queen of Erin put it on, and then the queen of Tubber Tintye said: " Tighten, belt ! " The belt tightened till the queen of Erin screamed with pain. " Now tell me," said the queen of Tubber Tintye, " who was the father of your elder son."

" The gardener," said the queen of Erin.

Again the queen of Tubber Tintye said: " Tighten, belt ! " The queen of Erin screamed worse than before; and she had good reason, for she was cut nearly in two. " Now tell me who was the father of your second son."

" The big brewer," said the queen of Erin.

Said the queen of Tubber Tintye to the king of Erin: " Get this woman dead."

The king put down a big fire then, and when it was blazing high, he threw the wife in, and she was destroyed at once.

" Now do you marry the queen of Lonesome Island, and my child will be grandchild to you and to her," said the queen of Tubber Tintye.

This was done, and the queen of Lonesome Island became queen of Erin and lived in the castle by the sea. And the queen of Tubber Tintye married the prince of Lonesome Island, the champion who entered the golden chamber while she slept.

Now the king of Erin sent ten ships with messages to all the kings of the world, inviting them to come to the wedding of the queen of Tubber Tintye and his son, and to his own wedding with the queen of Lonesome Island.

The queen removed the Druidic spells from her giants, beasts, and monsters; then went home, and made the prince of Lonesome Island king of Tubber Tintye and lord of the golden chamber.

THE SHEE AN GANNON AND THE GRUAGACH GAIRE.

THE Shee an Gannon [1] was born in the morning, named at noon, and went in the evening to ask his daughter of the king of Erin.

"I will give you my daughter in marriage," said the king of Erin; "you won't get her, though, unless you go and bring me back the tidings that I want, and tell me what it is that put a stop to the laughing of the Gruagach Gaire,[2] who before this laughed always, and laughed so loud that the whole world heard him. There are twelve iron spikes out here in the garden behind my castle. On eleven of the spikes are the heads of kings' sons who came seeking my daughter in marriage, and all of them went away to get the knowledge I wanted. Not one was able to get it and tell me what stopped the Gruagach Gaire from laughing. I took the heads off them all when they came back without the tidings for which they went, and I'm greatly in dread that your head'll be on the twelfth spike, for I'll do the same to you that I did to the eleven kings' sons unless you tell what put a stop to the laughing of the Gruagach."

The Shee an Gannon made no answer, but left the king and pushed away to know could he find why the Gruagach was silent.

He took a glen at a step, a hill at a leap, and

---

[1] Shee an Gannon, in Gaelic "Sighe an Gannon," the fairy of the Gannon.

[2] The laughing Gruagach.

travelled all day till evening. Then he came to a
house. The master of the house asked him what
sort was he, and he said: " A young man looking
for hire."

" Well," said the master of the house, " I was
going to-morrow to look for a man to mind my
cows. If you 'll work for me, you 'll have a good
place, the best food a man could have to eat in this
world, and a soft bed to lie on."

The Shee an Gannon took service, and ate his
supper. Then the master of the house said: " I
am the Gruagach Gaire; now that you are my
man and have eaten your supper, you 'll have a
bed of silk to sleep on."

Next morning after breakfast the Gruagach said
to the Shee an Gannon: " Go out now and loosen
my five golden cows and my bull without horns,
and drive them to pasture; but when you have
them out on the grass, be careful you don't let
them go near the land of the giant."

The new cowboy drove the cattle to pasture,
and when near the land of the giant, he saw it was
covered with woods and surrounded by a high
wall. He went up, put his back against the wall,
and threw in a great stretch of it; then he went
inside and threw out another great stretch of the
wall, and put the five golden cows and the bull
without horns on the land of the giant.

Then he climbed a tree, ate the sweet apples
himself, and threw the sour ones down to the
cattle of the Gruagach Gaire.

Soon a great crashing was heard in the woods,
— the noise of young trees bending, and old trees
breaking. The cowboy looked around, and saw a
five-headed giant pushing through the trees; and
soon he was before him.

" Poor miserable creature ! " said the giant;
" but were n't you impudent to come to my land
and trouble me in this way? You 're too big for
one bite, and too small for two. I don't know what
to do but tear you to pieces."

" You nasty brute," said the cowboy, coming
down to him from the tree, " 't is little I care for
you ; " and then they went at each other. So great
was the noise between them that there was nothing
in the world but what was looking on and listening
to the combat.

They fought till late in the afternoon, when the
giant was getting the upper hand; and then the
cowboy thought that if the giant should kill him,
his father and mother would never find him or set
eyes on him again, and he would never get the
daughter of the king of Erin. The heart in his
body grew strong at this thought. He sprang on
the giant, and with the first squeeze and thrust
he put him to his knees in the hard ground, with
the second thrust to his waist, and with the third
to his shoulders.

" I have you at last; you 're done for now ! " said
the cowboy. Then he took out his knife, cut the
five heads off the giant, and when he had them off
he cut out the tongues and threw the heads over
the wall.

Then he put the tongues in his pocket and
drove home the cattle. That evening the Gruagach could n't find vessels enough in all his place
to hold the milk of the five golden cows.

After supper the cowboy would give no talk to
his master, but kept his mind to himself, and went
to the bed of silk to sleep.

Next morning after breakfast the cowboy drove
out his cattle, and going on farther than the day

before, stopped at a high wall. He put his back to the wall, threw in a long stretch of it, then went in and threw out another long stretch of it.

After that he put the five golden cows and the bull without horns on the land, and going up on a tree, ate sweet apples himself, and threw down the sour ones to the cattle.

Now the son of the king of Tisean set out from the king of Erin on the same errand, after asking for his daughter; and as soon as the cowboy drove in his cattle on the second day, he came along by the giant's land, found the five heads of the giant thrown out by the cowboy the day before, and picking them up, ran off to the king of Erin and put them down before him.

" Oh, you have done good work ! " said the king. " You have won one third of my daughter."

Soon after the cowboy had begun to eat sweet apples, and the son of the king of Tisean had run off with the five heads, there came a great noise of young trees bending, and old trees breaking, and presently the cowboy saw a giant larger than the one he had killed the day before.

" You miserable little wretch ! " cried the giant; " what brings you here on my land? "

" You wicked brute ! " said the cowboy, " I don't care for you; " and slipping down from the tree, he fell upon the giant.

The fight was fiercer than his first one; but towards evening, when he was growing faint, the cowboy remembered that if he should fall, neither his father nor mother would see him again, and he would never get the daughter of the king of Erin.

This thought gave him strength; and jumping

up, he caught the giant, put him with one thrust to his knees in the hard earth, with a second to his waist, with a third to his shoulders, and then swept the five heads off him and threw them over the wall, after he had cut out the tongues and put them in his pocket.

Leaving the body of the giant, the cowboy drove home the cattle, and the Gruagach had still greater trouble in finding vessels for the milk of the five golden cows.

After supper the cowboy said not a word, but went to sleep.

Next morning he drove the cattle still farther, and came to green woods and a strong wall. Putting his back to the wall, he threw in a great piece of it, and going in, threw out another piece. Then he drove the five golden cows and the bull without horns to the land inside, ate sweet apples himself, and threw down sour ones to the cattle.

The son of the king of Tisean came and carried off the heads as on the day before.

Presently a third giant came crashing through the woods, and a battle followed more terrible than the other two.

Towards evening the giant was gaining the upper hand, and the cowboy, growing weak, would have been killed; but the thought of his parents and the daughter of the king of Erin gave him strength, and he swept the five heads off the giant, and threw them over the wall after he had put the tongues in his pocket.

Then the cowboy drove home his cattle; and the Gruagach did n't know what to do with the milk of the five golden cows, there was so much of it.

But when the cowboy was on the way home

with the cattle, the son of the king of Tisean came, took the five heads of the giant, and hurried to the king of Erin.

"You have won my daughter now," said the king of Erin when he saw the heads; "but you'll not get her unless you tell me what stops the Gruagach Gaire from laughing."

On the fourth morning the cowboy rose before his master, and the first words he said to the Gruagach were:

"What keeps you from laughing, you who used to laugh so loud that the whole world heard you?"

"I'm sorry," said the Gruagach, "that the daughter of the king of Erin sent you here."

"If you don't tell me of your own will, I'll make you tell me," said the cowboy; and he put a face on himself that was terrible to look at, and running through the house like a madman, could find nothing that would give pain enough to the Gruagach but some ropes made of untanned sheepskin hanging on the wall.

He took these down, caught the Gruagach, fastened his two hands behind him, and tied his feet so that his little toes were whispering to his ears. When he was in this state the Gruagach said: "I'll tell you what stopped my laughing if you set me free."

So the cowboy unbound him, the two sat down together, and the Gruagach said: —

"I lived in this castle here with my twelve sons. We ate, drank, played cards, and enjoyed ourselves, till one day when my sons and I were playing, a wizard hare came rushing in, jumped on our table, defiled it, and ran away.

"On another day he came again; but if he did,

we were ready for him, my twelve sons and myself. As soon as he defiled our table and ran off,
we made after him, and followed him till nightfall,
when he went into a glen. We saw a light before
us. I ran on, and came to a house with a great
apartment, where there was a man with twelve
daughters, and the hare was tied to the side of
the room near the women.

"There was a large pot over the fire in the
room, and a great stork boiling in the pot. The
man of the house said to me: 'There are bundles
of rushes at the end of the room, go there and sit
down with your men!'

"He went into the next room and brought out
two pikes, one of wood, the other of iron, and
asked me which of the pikes would I take. I
said, 'I'll take the iron one;' for I thought in my
heart that if an attack should come on me, I could
defend myself better with the iron than the wooden
pike.

"The man of the house gave me the iron pike,
and the first chance of taking what I could out of
the pot on the point of the pike. I got but a
small piece of the stork, and the man of the house
took all the rest on his wooden pike. We had
to fast that night; and when the man and his
twelve daughters ate the flesh of the stork, they
hurled the bare bones in the faces of my sons and
myself.

"We had to stop all night that way, beaten on
the faces by the bones of the stork.

"Next morning, when we were going away, the
man of the house asked me to stay a while; and
going into the next room, he brought out twelve
loops of iron and one of wood, and said to me:
'Put the heads of your twelve sons into the iron

loops, or your own head into the wooden one; '
and I said: ' I 'll put the twelve heads of my sons
in the iron loops, and keep my own out of the
wooden one.'

"He put the iron loops on the necks of my
twelve sons, and put the wooden one on his own
neck. Then he snapped the loops one after
another, till he took the heads off my twelve sons
and threw the heads and bodies out of the house;
but he did nothing to hurt his own neck.

"When he had killed my sons he took hold of
me and stripped the skin and flesh from the small
of my back down, and when he had done that he
took the skin of a black sheep that had been hanging on the wall for seven years and clapped it on
my body in place of my own flesh and skin; and
the sheepskin grew on me, and every year since
then I shear myself, and every bit of wool I use
for the stockings that I wear I clip off my own
back."

When he had said this, the Gruagach showed
the cowboy his back covered with thick black
wool.

After what he had seen and heard, the cowboy
said: "I know now why you don't laugh, and
small blame to you. But does that hare come
here still to spoil your table?"

"He does indeed," said the Gruagach.

Both went to the table to play, and they were
not long playing cards when the hare ran in; and
before they could stop him he was on the table,
and had put it in such a state that they could not
play on it longer if they had wanted to.

But the cowboy made after the hare, and the
Gruagach after the cowboy, and they ran as fast
as ever their legs could carry them till nightfall;

and when the hare was entering the castle where the twelve sons of the Gruagach were killed, the cowboy caught him by the two hind legs and dashed out his brains against the wall; and the skull of the hare was knocked into the chief room of the castle, and fell at the feet of the master of the place.

"Who has dared to interfere with my fighting pet?" screamed he.

"I," said the cowboy; "and if your pet had had manners, he might be alive now."

The cowboy and the Gruagach stood by the fire. A stork was boiling in the pot, as when the Gruagach came the first time. The master of the house went into the next room and brought out an iron and a wooden pike, and asked the cowboy which would he choose.

"I'll take the wooden one," said the cowboy; "and you may keep the iron one for yourself."

So he took the wooden one; and going to the pot, brought out on the pike all the stork except a small bite, and he and the Gruagach fell to eating, and they were eating the flesh of the stork all night. The cowboy and the Gruagach were at home in the place that time.

In the morning the master of the house went into the next room, took down the twelve iron loops with a wooden one, brought them out, and asked the cowboy which would he take, the twelve iron or the one wooden loop.

"What could I do with the twelve iron ones for myself or my master? I'll take the wooden one."

He put it on, and taking the twelve iron loops, put them on the necks of the twelve daughters of the house, then snapped the twelve heads off them, and turning to their father, said: "I'll do the same thing to you unless you bring the twelve sons of my master to life, and make them as well and strong as when you took their heads."

The master of the house went out and brought the twelve to life again; and when the Gruagach saw all his sons alive and as well as ever, he let a laugh out of himself, and all the Eastern world heard the laugh.

Then the cowboy said to the Gruagach: "It's a bad thing you have done to me, for the daughter of the king of Erin will be married the day after your laugh is heard."

"Oh! then we must be there in time," said the Gruagach; and they all made away from the place as fast as ever they could, the cowboy, the Gruagach, and his twelve sons.

On the road they came to a woman who was crying very hard.

"What is your trouble?" asked the cowboy.

"You need have no care," said she, "for I will not tell you."

"You must tell me," said he, "for I'll help you out of it."

"Well," said the woman, "I have three sons, and they used to play hurley with the three sons of the king of the Sasenach,[1] and they were more than a match for the king's sons. And it was the rule that the winning side should give three wallops of their hurleys to the other side; and my sons were winning every game, and gave such a beating to the king's sons that they complained to their father, and the king carried away my sons to London, and he is going to hang them there to-day."

"I'll bring them here this minute," said the cowboy.

---

[1] Sasenach, English.

" You have no time," said the Gruagach.

" Have you tobacco and a pipe?" asked the cowboy of the Gruagach.

" I have not," said he.

" Well, I have," said the cowboy; and putting his hand in his pocket, he took out tobacco and a pipe, gave them to the Gruagach, and said: " I 'll be in London and back before you can put tobacco in this pipe and light it."

He disappeared, was back from London with the three boys all safe and well, and gave them to their mother before the Gruagach could get a taste of smoke out of the pipe.

" Now come with us," said the cowboy to the woman and her sons, " to the wedding of the daughter of the king of Erin."

They hurried on; and when within three miles of the king's castle there was such a throng of people that no one could go a step ahead. " We must clear a road through this," said the cowboy.

" We must indeed," said the Gruagach; and at it they went, threw the people some on one side and some on the other, and soon they had an opening for themselves to the king's castle.

As they went in, the daughter of the king of Erin and the son of the king of Tisean were on their knees just going to be married. The cowboy drew his hand on the bridegroom, and gave a blow that sent him spinning till he stopped under a table at the other side of the room.

" What scoundrel struck that blow?" asked the king of Erin.

" It was I," said the cowboy.

" What reason had you to strike the man who won my daughter?"

" It was I who won your daughter, not he; and if you don't believe me, the Gruagach Gaire is here himself.   He'll tell you the whole story from beginning to end, and show you the tongues of the giants."

So the Gruagach came up and told the king the whole story, how the Shee an Gannon had become his cowboy, had guarded the five golden cows and the bull without horns, cut off the heads of the five-headed giants, killed the wizard hare, and brought his own twelve sons to life.   " And then," said the Gruagach, " he is the only man in the whole world I have ever told why I stopped laughing, and the only one who has ever seen my fleece of wool."

When the king of Erin heard what the Gruagach said, and saw the tongues of the giants fitted into the heads, he made the Shee an Gannon kneel down by his daughter, and they were married on the spot.

Then the son of the king of Tisean was thrown into prison, and the next day they put down a great fire, and the deceiver was burned to ashes.

The wedding lasted nine days, and the last day was better than the first.

THE THREE DAUGHTERS OF THE KING OF THE EAST, AND THE SON OF A KING IN ERIN.

THERE was once a king in Erin, and he had an only son. While this son was a little child his mother died.

After a time the king married and had a second son.

The two boys grew up together; and as the elder was far handsomer and better than the younger, the queen became jealous, and was for banishing him out of her sight.

The king's castle stood near the shore of Loch Erne, and three swans came every day to be in the water and swim in the lake. The elder brother used to go fishing; and once when he sat at the side of the water, the three swans made young women of themselves, came to where he sat, and talked to the king's son.

The queen had a boy minding cows in the place, and when he went home that night he told about what he had seen, — that there were three young women at the lake, and the king's son was talking to the three that day. Next morning the queen called the cowboy to her, and said: " Here is a pin of slumber; and do you stick it in the clothes of the king's son before the young women come, and when they go away, take out the pin and bring it back to me."

That day when the cowboy saw the three young

women coming, he went near and threw the pin, which stuck in the clothes of the king's son. That instant he fell asleep on the ground.

When the young women came, one of them took a towel, dipped it in the cold water of the lake, and rubbed his face; but she could not rouse him. When their time came to go, they were crying and lamenting because the young man was asleep; and one of the three put a gold pin in his bosom, so that when he woke up he would find it and keep her in mind.

After they had gone a couple of hours, the cowboy came up, took out the sleeping-pin, and hurried off. The king's son woke up without delay; and finding the gold pin in his bosom, he knew the young woman had come to see him.

Next day he fished and waited again. When the cowboy saw the young women coming out of the lake, he stole up a second time, and threw the pin, which stuck in his clothes, and that moment he was drowsy and fell asleep. When the young women came he was lying on the ground asleep. One of them rubbed him with a towel dipped in the water of the lake; but no matter what she did, he slept on, and when they had to go, she put a gold ring in his bosom. When the sisters were leaving the lake, and had put on their swan-skins and become swans, they all flew around him and flapped their wings in his face to know could they rouse him; but there was no use in trying.

After they had gone, the cowboy came and took out the sleeping-pin. When the king's son was awake he put his hand in his bosom, found the keepsake, and knew that the sisters had come to him.

When he went fishing the third day, he called up

the cowboy and said: " I fall asleep every day. I know something is done to me. Now do you tell me all. In time I 'll reward you well. I know my stepmother sends something by you that takes my senses away."

" I would tell," said the cowboy, " but I 'm in dread my mistress might kill or banish me."

" She will not, for I 'll put you in the way she 'll not harm you. You see my fishing-bag here? Now throw the pin, which I know you have, towards me, and hit the bag."

The cowboy did as he was told, and threw the pin into the fishing-bag, where it remained without harm to any one. The cowboy went back to his cattle, and the prince fished on as before. The three swans were out in the middle of the lake swimming around for themselves in the water, and the prince moved on, fishing, till he came to a bend in the shore. On one side of him a tongue of land ran out into the lake. The swans came to the shore, leaving the piece of land between themselves and the prince. Then they took off their swanskins, were young women, and bathed in the lake.

After that they came out, put on the dress of young women, and went to where the king's son was fishing.

He spoke to them, and asked where were they from, in what place were they born, and why were they swans.

They said: " We are three sisters, daughters of the king of the East, and we have two brothers. Our mother died, and our father married again, and had two other daughters; and these two are not so good looking nor so well favored as we, and their mother was in dread they would n't get such fine husbands as we, so she enchanted us, and now we are going about the world from lake to lake in the form of swans."

Then the eldest of the three sisters said to the king's son: "What kind are you, and where were you born?"

"I was born in Erin," said he; "and when I was a little boy my mother died, my father married again and had a second son, and that son was n't to the eye what I was, and my stepmother was for banishing me from my father's house because she thought her own son was not so good as I was, and I am fishing here every day by the lake to keep out of her sight."

"Well," said the eldest sister, "I thought you were a king's son, and so I came to you in my own form to know could we go on in the world together."

"I don't know yet what to do," said the king's son.

"Well, be sure of your mind to-morrow, for that will be the last day for me here."

When the cowboy was going home, the king's son gave him the sleeping-pin for the stepmother. When he had driven in the cattle, the cowboy told the queen that the young man had fallen asleep as on the two other days.

But there was an old witch in the place who was wandering about the lake that day. She saw everything, went to the queen, and told her how the three swans had made young women of themselves, and talked with her stepson.

When the queen heard the old witch, she fell into a terrible rage at the cowboy for telling her a lie, and banished him out of her sight forever. Then she got another cowboy, and sent him off with the sleeping-pin next day. When he came near the lake, the king's son tried to drive him off; but the cowboy threw the sleeping-pin into his clothes, and he fell down near the edge of the water without sight or sense.

The three sisters came, and found him sleeping. They rubbed him, and threw water on his face, but they could not wake him. And the three were lamenting sorely, for they had brought a swan's skin with them that day, so the king's son might make a swan of himself and fly away with them, for this was their last day at that place; but they could do nothing now, for he lay there dead asleep on the ground before them.

The eldest sister pulled out her handkerchief, and the falling tears dropped on it. Then she took a knife, and cut one of the nipples from her breast. The second sister wrote on the handkerchief: "Keep this in mind till you get more account from us." They put it in his bosom and went away.

As soon as the sisters had gone, the cowboy came, drew out the pin, and hurried away. The stepmother was always trying to banish the king's son, hoping that something might happen to him, and her own son be the heir. So now he went off and wandered away through Erin, always inquiring for the eldest sister, but never could find her.

At the end of seven years he came home, and was fishing at the side of Loch Erne again, when a swan flew up to him and said: "Your love is lying on her death-bed, unless you go to save her. She is bleeding from the breast, and you must go to her now. Go straight to the East!"

The king's son went straight to the East, and on the way there rose up storm and fog against him;

but they did not stop him. He was going on always, and when he was three weeks' journey from his father's castle he stumbled one dark, misty day and fell over a ditch. When he rose up there stood on the other side of the ditch before him a little horse, all bridled and saddled, with a whip on the saddle. The horse spoke up and said: " If you are the king's son, I was sent here to meet you, and carry you to the castle of the king of the East. There is a young woman at the castle who thinks it long till she sees you. Now ask me no questions, for I 'm not at liberty to talk to you till I bring you to the East."

" I suppose we are to be a long time going? " said the king's son.

" Don't trouble yourself about the going; I 'll take you safely. Sit on my back now, and be sure you 're a good rider, and you 'll not be long on the road. This is my last word."

They went on, and were going always; and as he travelled, the prince met the wind that was before him, and the wind that blew behind could not come up with him. When he was hungry the pommel of the saddle opened, and he found the best of eating inside.

They went on sweeping over the world for two weeks, and when they were near the East the horse said: " Get down from my back now, for it 's tired I am."

" How far are we from the castle? " asked the king's son.

" Five days' journey," answered the horse. "When you come to the castle, don't stop a moment till you ask where the young woman is lying; and tell them to be sure to give good stabling and food to the horse. Come and see me yourself every day. If you don't, there will be nothing for me but fasting; and that's what I don't like."

When the king's son came to the castle it was evening. The two younger sisters welcomed him. (These were two of the swans at the lake in Erin, and now at home by the enchantment of their step-mother. They were swans in the daytime, and women only at night, so as not to be under the eye of young men when these came to see the stepmother's own daughters.) They said: "Our sister is on an island, and we'll go to her." They got a boat for the young man, and went with him to where their sister was lying. They said to her: "The son of the king of Erin is here."

"Let him come in, that I may look at him," said she.

The king's son went in, and when she saw him she was glad. "Have you anything that belongs to me?" asked she.

"I have."

"Then throw it on my breast."

He threw the handkerchief on her breast and went away. Next day she rose from the bed as well as ever. On the third day after his arrival, the son of the king of Erin married the eldest daughter of the king of the East, and the step-mother's enchantment was destroyed; and there was the grandest wedding that ever was seen in that kingdom.

The king's son, thinking only of his bride, forgot all about the horse that had brought him over the long road. When at last he went to see him, the stable was empty; the horse had gone. And neither his father in Erin nor the stepmother came to his mind, he was living so pleasantly in the East.

But after he had been there a long time, and a son and a daughter had been born to him, he remembered his father. Then he made up his mind not to let the stepmother's son be heir to the kingdom in place of himself. So taking his wife and children, he left the East and travelled to Erin. He stopped on the road, and sent word to the father that he was coming.

When the stepmother heard the news, a great weakness came on her. She fell into a fit and died.

The king's son waited in a convenient place till the funeral was over, and then he came to the castle and lived with his father. He was not long in the place when he sent messengers to know could they find the cowboy that the stepmother banished for telling about the sleeping-pin. They brought the cowboy to the castle, and the king made him his coachman.

The cowboy was not twelve months in his new place before he married. Then the king's son gave him a fine piece of land to live on, with six cows and four horses. There was not a happier man in the kingdom than the cowboy. When the father died, the king's son became king in Erin himself.

THE FISHERMAN'S SON AND THE GRUAGACH OF TRICKS.

THERE was an old fisherman once in Erin who had a wife and one son.

The old fisherman used to go about with a fishing-rod and tackle to the rivers and lochs and every place where fish resort, and he was killing salmon and other fish to keep the life in himself and his wife and son.

The son was not so keen nor so wise as another, and the father was instructing him every day in fishing, so that if himself should be taken from the world, the son would be able to support the old mother and get his own living.

One day when the father and son were fishing in a river near the sea, they looked out over the water and saw a small dark speck on the waves. It grew larger and larger, till they saw a boat, and when the boat drew near they saw a man sitting in the stern of it.

There was a nice beach near the place where they were fishing. The man brought the boat straight to the beach, and stepping out drew it up on the sand.

They saw then that the stranger was a man of high degree (*duine uasal*).

After he had put the boat high on the sand, he came to where the two were at work, and said: "Old fisherman, you 'd better let this son of yours with me for a year and a day, and I will make a very wise man of him. I am the Gruagach na g-cleasan[1] (Gruagach of tricks), and I'll bind myself to be here with your son this day year."

"I can't let him go," said the old fisherman, "till he gets his mother's advice."

"Whatever goes as far as women I'll have nothing to do with," said the Gruagach. "You had better give him to me now, and let the mother alone."

They talked till at last the fisherman promised to let his son go for the year and a day. Then the Gruagach gave his word to have the boy there at the seashore that day year.

The Gruagach and the boy went into the boat and sailed away.

When the year and a day were over, the old fisherman went to the same place where he had parted with his son and the Gruagach, and stood looking over the sea, thinking would he see his son that day.

At last he saw a black spot on the water, then a boat. When it was near he saw two men sitting in the stern of the boat. When it touched land, the two, who were *duine uasal* in appearance, jumped out, and one of them pulled the boat to the top of the strand. Then that one, followed by the other, came to where the old fisherman was waiting, and asked: "What trouble is on you now, my good man?"

"I had a son that wasn't so keen nor so wise as another, and myself and this son were here fishing, and a stranger came, like yourself to-day, and asked would I let my son with him for a year and a day. I let the son go, and the man promised to be here with him to-day, and that's why I am waiting at this place now."

---

[1] Pronounced ná glássan.

" Well," said the Gruagach, " am I your son? "

" You are not," said the fisherman.

" Is this man here your son? "

" I don't know him," said the fisherman.

" Well, then, he is all you will have in place of your son," said the Gruagach.

The old man looked again, and knew his son. He caught hold of him and welcomed him home.

" Now," said the Gruagach, " is n't he a better man than he was a year ago? "

" Oh, he 's nearly a smart man now! " said the old fisherman.

" Well," said the Gruagach, " will you let him with me for another year and a day? "

" I will not," said the old man; " I want him myself."

The Gruagach then begged and craved till the fisherman promised to let the son with him for a year and a day again. . But the old man forgot to take his word of the Gruagach to bring back the son at the end of the time ; and when the Gruagach and the boy were in the boat, and had pushed out to sea, the Gruagach shouted to the old man : " I kept my promise to bring back your son to-day. I have n't given you my word at all now. I 'll not bring him back, and you 'll never see him again."

The fisherman went home with a heavy and sorrowful heart, and the old woman scolded him all that night till next morning for letting her son go with the Gruagach a second time.

Then himself and the old woman were lamenting a quarter of a year; and when another quarter had passed, he said to her : " I 'll leave you here now, and I 'll be walking on myself till I wear my legs off up to my knees, and from my knees to my waist, till I find where is my son."

So away went the old man walking, and he used to spend but one night in a house, and not two nights in any house, till his feet were all in blisters. One evening late he came to a hut where there was an old woman sitting at a fire.

" Poor man ! " said she, when she laid eyes on him, " it's a great distress you are in, to be so disfigured with wounds and sores. What is the trouble that's on you ? "

" I had a son," said the old man, " and the Gruagach na g-cleasan came on a day and took him from me."

" Oh, poor man ! " said she. " I have a son with that same Gruagach these twelve years, and I have never been able to get him back or get sight of him, and I'm in dread you'll not be able to get your son either. But to-morrow, in the morning, I'll tell you all I know, and show you the road you must go to find the house of the Gruagach na g-cleasan."

Next morning she showed the old fisherman the road. He was to come to the place by evening.

When he came and entered the house, the Gruagach shook hands with him, and said: " You are welcome, old fisherman. It was I that put this journey on you, and made you come here looking for your son."

" It was no one else but you," said the fisherman.

" Well," said the Gruagach, " you won't see your son to-day. At noon to-morrow I'll put a whistle in my mouth and call together all the birds in my place, and they'll come. Among others will be twelve doves. I'll put my hand in my pocket, this way, and take out wheat and throw it before them on the ground. The doves will eat the wheat, and you must pick your son out of the twelve. If you find him, you'll have him; if you don't, you'll never get him again."

After the Gruagach had said these words the old man ate his supper and went to bed.

In the dead of night the old fisherman's son came. "Oh, father!" said he, "it would be hard for you to pick me out among the twelve doves, if you had to do it alone; but I'll tell you. When the Gruagach calls us in, and we go to pick up the wheat, I'll make a ring around the others, walking for myself; and as I go I'll give some of them a tip of my bill, and I'll lift my wings when I'm striking them. There was a spot under one of my arms when I left home, and you'll see that spot under my wing when I raise it to-morrow. Don't miss the bird that I'll be, and don't let your eyes off it; if you do, you'll lose me forever."

Next morning the old man rose, had his breakfast, and kept thinking of what his son had told him.

At midday the Gruagach took his whistle and blew. Birds came to him from every part, and among others the twelve doves.

He took wheat from his pocket, threw it to the doves, and said to the father: "Now pick out your son from the twelve."

The old man was watching, and soon he saw one of the doves walking around the other eleven and hitting some of them a clip of its bill, and then it raised its wings, and the old man saw the spot. The bird let its wings down again, and went to eating with the rest.

The father never let his eyes off the bird. After a while he said to the Gruagach: "I'll have that bird there for my son."

"Well," said the Gruagach, "that is your son. I can't blame you for having him; but I blame your instructor for the information he gave you, and I give him my curse."

So the old fisherman got his son back in his proper shape, and away they went, father and son, from the house of the Gruagach. The old man felt stronger now, and they never stopped travelling a day till they came home.

The old mother was very glad to see her son, and see him such a wise, smart man.

After coming home they had no means but the fishing; they were as poor as ever before.

At this time it was given out at every cross-road in Erin, and in all public places in the kingdom, that there were to be great horse-races. Now, when the day came, the old fisherman's son said:

"Come away with me, father, to the races."

The old man went with him, and when they were near the race-course, the son said: "Stop here till I tell you this: I'll make myself into the best horse that's here to-day, and do you take me to the place where the races are to be, and when you take me in, I'll open my mouth, trying to kill and eat every man that'll be near me, I'll have such life and swiftness; and do you find a rider for me that'll ride me, and don't let me go till the other horses are far ahead on the course. Then let me go. I'll come up to them, and I'll run ahead of them and win the race. After that every rich man there will want to buy me of you; but don't you sell me to any man for less than five hundred pounds; and be sure you get that price for me. And when you have the gold, and you are giving me up, take the bit out of my mouth, and don't sell the bridle for any money. Then come to this spot, shake the bridle, and I'll be here in my own form before you."

The son made himself a horse, and the old fisherman took him to the race. He reared and snorted, trying to take the head off every man that came near him.

The old man shouted for a rider. A rider came; he mounted the horse and held him in. The old man didn't let him start till the other horses were well ahead on the course; then he let him go.

The new horse caught up with the others and shot past them. So they had not gone half way when he was in at the winning-post.

When the race was ended, there was a great noise over the strange horse. Men crowded around the old fisherman from every corner of the field, asking what would he take for the horse.

" Five hundred pounds," said he.

" Here 't is for you," said the next man to him.

In a moment the horse was sold, and the money in the old man's pocket. Then he pulled the bridle off the horse's head, and made his way out of the place as fast as ever he could.

It was not long till he was at the spot where the son had told him what to do. The minute he came, he shook the bridle, and the son was there before him in his own shape and features.

Oh, but the old fisherman was glad when he had his son with him again, and the money in his pocket!

The two went home together. They had money enough now to live, and quit the fishing. They had plenty to eat and drink, and they spent their lives in ease and comfort till the next year, when it was given out at all the cross-roads in Erin, and every public place in the kingdom, that there was to be a great hunting with hounds, in the same place where the races had been the year before.

When the day came, the fisherman's son said: " Come, father, let us go away to this hunting."

" Ah ! " said the old man, " what do we want to go for? Have n't we plenty to eat at home, with money enough and to spare? What do we care for hunting with hounds?"

" Oh! they 'll give us more money," said the son, " if we go."

The fisherman listened to his son, and away they went. When the two came to the spot where the son had made a horse of himself the year before, he stopped, and said to the father: " I 'll make a hound of myself to-day, and when you bring me in sight of the game, you 'll see me wild with jumping and trying to get away; but do you hold me fast till the right time comes, then let go. I 'll sweep ahead of every hound in the field, catch the game, and win the prize for you.

" When the hunt is over, so many men will come to buy me that they 'll put you in a maze; but be sure you get three hundred pounds for me, and when you have the money, and are giving me up, don't forget to keep my rope. Come to this place, shake the rope, and I 'll be here before you, as I am now. If you don't keep the rope, you 'll go home without me."

The son made a hound of himself, and the old father took him to the hunting-ground.

When the hunt began, the hound was springing and jumping like mad; but the father held him till the others were far out in the field. Then he let him loose, and away went the son.

Soon he was up with the pack, then in front of

the pack, and never stopped till he caught the game and won the prize.

When the hunt was over, and the dogs and game brought in, all the people crowded around the old fisherman, saying: " What do you want of that hound? Better sell him; he's no good to you."

They put the old man in a maze, there were so many of them, and they pressed him so hard.

He said at last: " I'll sell the hound; and three hundred pounds is the price I want for him."

" Here 't is for you," said a stranger, putting the money into his hand.

The old man took the money and gave up the dog, without taking off the rope. He forgot his son's warning.

That minute the Gruagach na g-cleasan called out: " I'll take the worth of my money out of your son now; " and away he went with the hound.

The old man walked home alone that night, and it is a heavy heart he had in him when he came to the old woman without the son. And the two were lamenting their lot till morning.

Still and all, they were better off than the first time they lost their son, as they had plenty of everything, and could live at their ease.

The Gruagach went away home, and put the fisherman's son in a cave of concealment that he had, bound him hand and foot, and tied hard knots on his neck up to the chin. From above there fell on him drops of poison, and every drop that fell went from the skin to the flesh, from the flesh to the bone, from the bone to the marrow, and he sat there under the poison drops, without meat, drink, or rest.

In the Gruagach's house was a servant-maid, and the fisherman's son had been kind to her the time he was in the place before.

On a day when the Gruagach and his eleven sons were out hunting, the maid was going with a tub of dirty water to throw it into the river that ran by the side of the house. She went through the cave of concealment where the fisherman's son was bound, and he asked of her the wetting of his mouth from the tub.

" Oh! the Gruagach would take the life of me," said she, " when he comes home, if I gave you as much as one drop."

" Well," said he, " when I was in this house before, and when I had power in my hands, it's good and kind I was to you; and when I get out of this confinement I'll do you a turn, if you give me the wetting of my mouth now."

The maid put the tub near his lips.

" Oh! I can't stoop to drink unless you untie one knot from my throat," said he.

Then she put the tub down, stooped to him, and loosed one knot from his throat. When she loosed the one knot he made an eel of himself, and dropped into the tub. There he began shaking the water, till he put some of it on the ground, and when he had the place about him wet, he sprang from the tub, and slipped along out under the door. The maid caught him; but could not hold him, he was so slippery. He made his way from the door to the river, which ran near the side of the house.

When the Gruagach na g-cleàsan came home in the evening with his eleven sons, they went to take a look at the fisherman's son; but he was not to be seen.

Then the Gruagach called the maid, and taking his sword, said: " I 'll take the head off you if you don't tell me this minute what happened while I was gone."

" Oh!" said the maid, " he begged so hard for a drop of dirty water to wet his mouth that I had n't the heart to refuse, for 't is good he was to me and kind each time he saw me when he was here in the house before. When the water touched his mouth, he made an eel of himself, spilled water out of the tub, and slipped along over the wet place to the river outside. I caught him to bring him back, but I could n't hold him; in spite of all I could do, he made away."

The Gruagach dropped his sword, and went to the water side with his sons.

The sons made eleven eels of themselves, and the Gruagach their father was the twelfth. They went around in the water, searching in every place, and there was not a stone in the river that they passed without looking under and around it for the old fisherman's son.

And when he knew that they were after him, he made himself into a salmon; and when they knew he was a salmon, the sons made eleven otters of themselves, and the Gruagach made himself the twelfth.

When the fisherman's son found that twelve otters were after him, he was weak with hunger, and when they had come near, he made himself a whale. But the eleven brothers and their father made twelve cannon whales of themselves, for they had all gone out of the river, and were in the sea now.

When they were coming near him, the fisherman's son was weak from pursuit and hunger, so he jumped up out of the water, and made a swallow of himself; but the Gruagach and his sons became twelve hawks, and chased the swallow through the air; and as they whirled round and darted, they pressed him hard, till all of them came near the castle of the king of Erin.

Now the king had made a summer-house for his daughter; and where should she be at this time but sitting on the top of the summer-house.

The old fisherman's son dropped down till he was near her; then he fell into her lap in the form of a ring. The daughter of the king of Erin took up the ring, looked at it, and put it on her finger. The ring took her fancy, and she was glad.

When the Gruagach and his sons saw this, they let themselves down at the king's castle, having the form of the finest men that could be seen in the kingdom.

When the king's daughter had the ring on her finger she looked at it and liked it. Then the ring spoke, and said: " My life is in your hands now; don't part from the ring, and don't let it go to any man, and you 'll give me a long life."

The Gruagach na g-cleasan and his eleven sons went into the king's castle and played on every instrument known to man, and they showed every sport that could be shown before a king. This they did for three days and three nights. When that time was over, and they were going away, the king spoke up and asked:

" What is the reward that you would like, and what would be pleasing to you from me? "

" We want neither gold nor silver," said the Gruagach; " all the reward we ask of you is the ring that I lost on a time, and which is now on your daughter's finger."

"If my daughter has the ring that you lost, it shall be given to you," said the king.

Now the ring spoke to the king's daughter and said: "Don't part with me for anything till you send your trusted man for three gallons of strong spirits and a gallon of wheat; put the spirits and the wheat together in an open barrel before the fire. When your father says you must give up the ring, do you answer back that you have never left the summer-house, that you have nothing on your hand but what is your own and paid for. Your father will say then that you must part with me, and give me up to the stranger. When he forces you in this way, and you can keep me no longer, then throw me into the fire; and you'll see great sport and strange things."

The king's daughter sent for the spirits and the wheat, had them mixed together, and put in an open barrel before the fire.

The king called the daughter in, and asked: "Have you the ring which this stranger lost?"

"I have a ring," said she, "but it's my own, and I'll not part with it. I'll not give it to him nor to any man."

"You must," said the king, "for my word is pledged, and you must part with the ring!"

When she heard this, she slipped the ring from her finger and threw it into the fire.

That moment the eleven brothers made eleven pairs of tongs of themselves; their father, the old Gruagach, was the twelfth pair.

The twelve jumped into the fire to know in what spark of it would they find the old fisherman's son; and they were a long time working and searching through the fire, when out flew a spark, and into the barrel.

The twelve made themselves men, turned over the barrel, and spilled the wheat on the floor. Then in a twinkling they were twelve cocks strutting around.

They fell to and picked away at the wheat to know which one would find the fisherman's son. Soon one dropped on one side, and a second on the opposite side, until all twelve were lying drunk from the wheat.

Then the old fisherman's son made a fox of himself, and the first cock he came to was the old Gruagach na g-cleasan himself. He took the head off the Gruagach with one bite, and the heads off the eleven brothers with eleven other bites.

When the twelve were dead, the old fisherman's son made himself the finest-looking man in Erin, and began to give music and sport to the king; and he entertained him five times better than had the Gruagach and his eleven sons.

Then the king's daughter fell in love with him, and she set her mind on him to that degree that there was no life for her without him.

When the king saw the straits that his daughter was in, he ordered the marriage without delay.

The wedding lasted for nine days and nine nights, and the ninth night was the best of all.

When the wedding was over, the king felt he was losing his strength, so he took the crown off his own head, and put it on the head of the old fisherman's son, and made him king of Erin in place of himself.

The young couple were the luck, and we the stepping-stones. The presents we got at the marriage were stockings of buttermilk and shoes of paper, and these were worn to the soles of our feet when we got home from the wedding.

THE THIRTEENTH SON OF THE KING OF ERIN.

THERE was a king in Erin long ago who had thirteen sons, and as they grew up he taught them good learning and every exercise and art befitting their rank.

One day the king went hunting, and saw a swan swimming in a lake with thirteen little ones. She kept driving away the thirteenth, and would not let it come near the others.

The king wondered greatly at this, and when he came home he summoned his Sean dall Glic (old blind sage), and said: "I saw a great wonder to-day while out hunting, — a swan with thirteen cygnets, and she driving away the thirteenth continually, and keeping the twelve with her. Tell me the cause and reason of this. Why should a mother hate her thirteenth little one, and guard the other twelve?"

"I will tell you," said the old blind sage: "all creatures on earth, whether beast or human, which have thirteen young, should put the thirteenth away, and let it wander for itself through the world and find its fate, so that the will of Heaven may work upon it, and not come down on the others. Now you have thirteen sons, and you must give the thirteenth to the Diachbha." [1]

[1] Diachbha, "divinity," "fate."

" Then that is the meaning of the swan on the lake, — I must give up my thirteenth son to the Diachbha? "

" It is," said the old blind sage; " you must give up one of your thirteen sons."

" But how can I give one of them away when I am so fond of all; and which one shall it be? "

" I 'll tell you what to do. When the thirteen come home to-night, shut the door against the last that comes."

Now one of the sons was slow, not so keen nor so sharp as another; but the eldest, who was called Sean Ruadh, was the best, the hero of them all. And it happened that night that he came home last, and when he came his father shut the door against him. The boy raised his hands and said: " Father, what are you going to do with me; what do you wish? "

" It is my duty," said the father, " to give one of my sons to the Diachbha; and as you are the thirteenth, you must go."

" Well, give me my outfit for the road."

The outfit was brought, Sean Ruadh put it on; then the father gave him a black-haired steed that could overtake the wind before him, and outstrip the wind behind.

Sean Ruadh mounted the steed and hurried away. He went on each day without rest, and slept in the woods at night.

One morning he put on some old clothes which he had in a pack on the saddle, and leaving his horse in the woods, went aside to an opening. He was not long there when a king rode up and stopped before him.

" Who are you, and where are you going? " asked the king.

" Oh! " said Sean Ruadh, " I am astray. I do not know where to go, nor what I am to do."

" If that is how you are, I'll tell you what to do, — come with me."

" Why should I go with you? " asked Sean Ruadh.

" Well, I have a great many cows, and I have no one to go with them, no one to mind them. I am in great trouble also. My daughter will die a terrible death very soon."

" How will she die? " asked Sean Ruadh.

" There is an urfeist,[1] a great serpent of the sea, a monster which must get a king's daughter to devour every seven years. Once in seven years this thing comes up out of the sea for its meat. The turn has now come to my daughter, and we don't know what day will the urfeist appear. The whole castle and all of us are in mourning for my wretched child."

" Perhaps some one will come to save her," said Sean Ruadh.

" Oh! there is a whole army of kings' sons who have come, and they all promise to save her; but I'm in dread none of them will meet the urfeist."

Sean Ruadh agreed with the king to serve for seven years, and went home with him.

Next morning Sean Ruadh drove out the king's cows to pasture.

Now there were three giants not far from the king's place. They lived in three castles in sight of each other, and every night each of these giants shouted just before going to bed. So loud was the shout that each let out of himself that the people heard it in all the country around.

Sean Ruadh drove the cattle up to the giant's

[1] Urfeist, "great serpent."

land, pushed down the wall, and let them in. The grass was very high, — three times better than any on the king's pastures.

As Sean Ruadh sat watching the cattle, a giant came running towards him and called out: " I don't know whether to put a pinch of you in my nose, or a bite of you in my mouth ! "

" Bad luck to me," said Sean Ruadh, " if I came here but to take the life out of you ! "

" How would you like to fight, — on the gray stones, or with sharp swords ? " asked the giant.

" I 'll fight you," said Sean Ruadh, " on the gray stones, where your great legs will be going down, and mine standing high."

They faced one another then, and began to fight. At the first encounter Sean Ruadh put the giant down to his knees among the hard gray stones, at the second he put him to his waist, and at the third to his shoulders.

" Come, take me out of this," cried the giant, " and I 'll give you my castle and all I 've got. I 'll give you my sword of light that never fails to kill at a blow. I 'll give you my black horse that can overtake the wind before, and outstrip the wind behind. These are all up there in my castle."

Sean Ruadh killed the giant and went up to the castle, where the housekeeper said to him: " Oh ! it is you that are welcome. You have killed the dirty giant that was here. Come with me now till I show you all the riches and treasures."

She opened the door of the giant's store-room and said: " All these are yours. Here are the keys of the castle."

" Keep them till I come again, and wake me in

the evening," said Sean Ruadh, lying down on the giant's bed.

He slept till evening; then the housekeeper roused him, and he drove the king's cattle home. The cows never gave so much milk as that night. They gave as much as in a whole week before.

Sean Ruadh met the king, and asked: "What news from your daughter?"

"The great serpent did not come to-day," said the king; "but he may come to-morrow."

"Well, to-morrow he may not come till another day," said Sean Ruadh.

Now the king knew nothing of the strength of Sean Ruadh, who was bare-footed, ragged, and shabby.

The second morning Sean Ruadh put the king's cows in the second giant's land. Out came the second giant with the same questions and threats as the first, and the cowboy spoke as on the day before.

They fell to fighting; and when the giant was to his shoulders in the hard gray rocks, he said: "I'll give you my sword of light and my brown-haired horse if you'll spare my life."

"Where is your sword of light?" asked Sean Ruadh.

"It is hung up over my bed."

Sean Ruadh ran to the giant's castle, and took the sword, which screamed out when he seized it; but he held it fast, hurried back to the giant, and asked, "How shall I try the edge of this sword?"

"Against a stick," was the reply.

"I see no stick better than your own head," said Sean Ruadh; and with that he swept the head off the giant.

The cowboy now went back to the castle and

hung up the sword. " Blessing to you," said the housekeeper; "you have killed the giant! Come, now, and I'll show you his riches and treasures, which are yours forever."

Sean Ruadh found more treasure in this castle than in the first one. When he had seen all, he gave the keys to the housekeeper till he should need them. He slept as on the day before, then drove the cows home in the evening.

The king said: "I have *the* luck since you came to me. My cows give three times as much milk to-day as they did yesterday."

"Well," said Sean Ruadh, " have you any account of the urfeist? "

" He didn't come to-day," said the king; " but he may come to-morrow."

Sean Ruadh went out with the king's cows on the third day, and drove them to the third giant's land, who came out and fought a more desperate battle than either of the other two; but the cowboy pushed him down among the gray rocks to his shoulders and killed him.

At the castle of the third giant he was received with gladness by the housekeeper, who showed him the treasures and gave him the keys; but he left the keys with her till he should need them. That evening the king's cows had more milk than ever before.

On the fourth day Sean Ruadh went out with the cows, but stopped at the first giant's castle. The housekeeper at his command brought out the dress of the giant, which was all black. He put on the giant's apparel, black as night, and girded on his sword of light. Then he mounted the black-haired steed, which overtook the wind before, and outstripped the wind behind; and rushing on be-

tween earth and sky, he never stopped till he came
to the beach, where he saw hundreds upon hundreds of kings' sons, and champions, who were
anxious to save the king's daughter, but were so
frightened at the terrible urfeist that they would
not go near her.

When he had seen the princess and the trembling champions, Sean Ruadh turned his black
steed to the castle.   Presently the king saw, riding
between earth and sky, a splendid stranger, who
stopped before him.

" What is that I see on the shore? " asked the
stranger.   " Is it a fair, or some great meeting? "

" Have n't you heard," asked the king, " that
a monster is coming to destroy my daughter
to-day? "

" No, I have n't heard anything," answered the
stranger, who turned away and disappeared.

Soon the black horseman was before the princess, who was sitting alone on a rock near the sea.
As she looked at the stranger, she thought he
was the finest man on earth, and her heart was
cheered.

" Have you no one to save you? " he asked.

" No one."

" Will you let me lay my head on your lap till
the urfeist comes?   Then rouse me."

He put his head on her lap and fell asleep.
While he slept, the princess took three hairs from
his head and hid them in her bosom.   As soon
as she had hidden the hairs, she saw the urfeist
coming on the sea, great as an island, and throwing
up water to the sky as he moved.   She roused the
stranger, who sprang up to defend her.

The urfeist came upon shore, and was advan-
cing on the princess with mouth open and wide

as a bridge, when the stranger stood before him
and said: " This woman is mine, not yours ! "

Then drawing his sword of light, he swept off
the monster's head with a blow; but the head
rushed back to its place, and grew on again.

In a twinkle the urfeist turned and went back
to the sea; but as he went, he said: " I 'll be
here again to-morrow, and swallow the whole world
before me as I come."

" Well," answered the stranger, " maybe another
will come to meet you."

Sean Ruadh mounted his black steed, and was
gone before the princess could stop him. Sad
was her heart when she saw him rush off between
the earth and sky more swiftly than any wind.

Sean Ruadh went to the first giant's castle and
put away his horse, clothes, and sword. Then he
slept on the giant's bed till evening, when the
housekeeper woke him, and he drove home the
cows. Meeting the king, he asked: " Well, how
has your daughter fared to-day? "

" Oh! the urfeist came out of the sea to carry
her away; but a wonderful black champion came
riding between earth and sky and saved her."

" Who was he? "

" Oh! there is many a man who says he did it.
But my daughter is n't saved yet, for the urfeist
said he 'd come to-morrow."

" Well, never fear; perhaps another champion
will come to-morrow."

Next morning Sean Ruadh drove the king's
cows to the land of the second giant, where he
left them feeding, and then went to the castle,
where the housekeeper met him and said: " You
are welcome. I 'm here before you, and all is
well."

" Let the brown horse be brought; let the giant's apparel and sword be ready for me," said Sean Ruadh.

The apparel was brought, the beautiful blue dress of the second giant, and his sword of light. Sean Ruadh put on the apparel, took the sword, mounted the brown steed, and sped away between earth and air three times more swiftly than the day before.

He rode first to the seashore, saw the king's daughter sitting on the rock alone, and the princes and champions far away, trembling in dread of the urfeist.   Then he rode to the king, enquired about the crowd on the seashore, and received the same answer as before. " But is there no man to save her? " asked Sean Ruadh.

" Oh! there are men enough," said the king, " who promise to save her, and say they are brave ; but there is no man of them who will stand to his word and face the urfeist when he rises from the sea."

Sean Ruadh was away before the king knew it, and rode to the princess in his suit of blue, bearing his sword of light. " Is there no one to save you? " asked he.

" No one."

" Let me lay my head on your lap, and when the urfeist comes, rouse me."

He put his head on her lap, and while he slept she took out the three hairs, compared them with his hair, and said to herself: " You are the man who was here yesterday."

When the urfeist appeared, coming over the sea, the princess roused the stranger, who sprang up and hurried to the beach.

The monster, moving at a greater speed, and

raising more water than on the day before, came with open mouth to land. Again Sean Ruadh stood in his way, and with one blow of the giant's sword made two halves of the urfeist. But the two halves rushed together, and were one as before.

Then the urfeist turned to the sea again, and said as he went: "All the champions on earth won't save her from me to-morrow!"

Sean Ruadh sprang to his steed and back to the castle. He went, leaving the princess in despair at his going. She tore her hair and wept for the loss of the blue champion, — the one man who had dared to save her.

Sean Ruadh put on his old clothes, and drove home the cows as usual. The king said: "A strange champion, all dressed in blue, saved my daughter to-day; but she is grieving her life away because he is gone."

"Well, that is a small matter, since her life is safe," said Sean Ruadh.

There was a feast for the whole world that night at the king's castle, and gladness was on every face that the king's daughter was safe again.

Next day Sean Ruadh drove the cows to the third giant's pasture, went to the castle, and told the housekeeper to bring the giant's sword and apparel, and have the red steed led to the door. The third giant's dress had as many colors as there are in the sky, and his boots were of blue glass.

Sean Ruadh, dressed and mounted on his red steed, was the most beautiful man in the world. When ready to start, the housekeeper said to him: "The beast will be so enraged this time that no arms can stop him; he will rise from the sea with three great swords coming out of his mouth, and he could cut to pieces and swallow the whole world if it stood before him in battle. There is only one way to conquer the urfeist, and I will show it to you. Take this brown apple, put it in your bosom, and when he comes rushing from the sea with open mouth, do you throw the apple down his throat, and the great urfeist will melt away and die on the strand."

Sean Ruadh went on the red steed between earth' and sky, with thrice the speed of the day before. He saw the maiden sitting on the rock alone, saw the trembling kings' sons in the distance watching to know what would happen, and saw the king hoping for some one to save his daughter; then he went to the princess, and put his head on her lap; when he had fallen asleep, she took the three hairs from her bosom, and looking at them, said: "You are the man who saved me yesterday."

The urfeist was not long in coming. The princess roused Sean Ruadh, who sprang to his feet and went to the sea. The urfeist came up enormous, terrible to look at, with a mouth big enough to swallow the world, and three sharp swords coming out of it. When he saw Sean Ruadh, he sprang at him with a roar; but Sean Ruadh threw the apple into his mouth, and the beast fell helpless on the strand, flattened out and melted away to a dirty jelly on the shore.

Then Sean Ruadh went towards the princess and said: "That urfeist will never trouble man or woman again."

The princess ran and tried to cling to him; but he was on the red steed, rushing away between earth and sky, before she could stop him. She held, however, so firmly to one of the blue glass boots that Sean Ruadh had to leave it in her hands.

When he drove home the cows that night, the

king came out, and Sean Ruadh asked: "What news from the urfeist?"

"Oh!" said the king, "I've had the luck since you came to me. A champion wearing all the colors of the sky, and riding a red steed between earth and air, destroyed the urfeist to-day. My daughter is safe forever; but she is ready to kill herself because she hasn't the man that saved her."

That night there was a feast in the king's castle such as no one had ever seen before. The halls were filled with princes and champions, and each one said: "I am the man that saved the princess!"

The king sent for the old blind sage, and asked, what should he do to find the man who saved his daughter. The old blind sage said, —

"Send out word to all the world that the man whose foot the blue glass boot will fit is the champion who killed the urfeist, and you'll give him your daughter in marriage."

The king sent out word to the world to come to try on the boot. It was too large for some, too small for others. When all had failed, the old sage said, —

"All have tried the boot but the cowboy."

"Oh! he is always out with the cows; what use in his trying," said the king.

"No matter," answered the old blind sage; "let twenty men go and bring down the cowboy."

The king sent up twenty men, who found the cowboy sleeping in the shadow of a stone wall. They began to make a hay rope to bind him; but he woke up, and had twenty ropes ready before they had one. Then he jumped at them, tied the twenty in a bundle, and fastened the bundle to the wall.

They waited and waited at the castle for the twenty men and the cowboy, till at last the king sent twenty men more, with swords, to know what was the delay.

When they came, this twenty began to make a hay rope to tie the cowboy; but he had twenty ropes made before their one, and no matter how they fought, the cowboy tied the twenty in a bundle, and the bundle to the other twenty men.

When neither party came back, the old blind sage said to the king: " Go up now, and throw yourself down before the cowboy, for he has tied the forty men in two bundles, and the bundles to each other."

The king went and threw himself down before the cowboy, who raised him up and said: " What is this for? "

" Come down now and try on the glass boot," said the king.

" How can I go, when I have work to do here ? "

" Oh! never mind; you 'll come back soon enough to do the work."

The cowboy untied the forty men and went down with the king. When he stood in front of the castle, he saw the princess sitting in her upper chamber, and the glass boot on the window-sill before her.

That moment the boot sprang from the window through the air to him, and went on his foot of itself. The princess was downstairs in a twinkle, and in the arms of Sean Ruadh.

The whole place was crowded with kings' sons and champions, who claimed that they had saved the princess.

" What are these men here for? " asked Sean Ruadh.

" Oh ! they have been trying to put on the boot," said the king.

With that Sean Ruadh drew his sword of light, swept the heads off every man of them, and threw heads and bodies on the dirt-heap behind the castle.

Then the king sent ships with messengers to all the kings and queens of the world, — to the kings of Spain, France, Greece, and Lochlin, and to Diarmuid, son of the monarch of light, — to come to the wedding of his daughter and Sean Ruadh.

Sean Ruadh, after the wedding, went with his wife to live in the kingdom of the giants, and left his father-in-law on his own land.

KIL ARTHUR.

THERE was a time long ago, and if we had lived then, we should n't be living now.

In that time there was a law in the world that if a young man came to woo a young woman, and her people would n't give her to him, the young woman should get her death by the law.

There was a king in Erin at that time who had a daughter, and he had a son too, who was called Kil Arthur, son of the monarch of Erin.

Now, not far from the castle of the king there was a tinker; and one morning he said to his mother: "Put down my breakfast for me, mother."

"Where are you going?" asked the mother.

"I'm going for a wife."

"Where?"

"I am going for the daughter of the king of Erin."

"Oh! my son, bad luck is upon you. It is death to ask for the king's daughter, and you a tinker."

"I don't care for that," said he.

So the tinker went to the king's castle. They were at dinner when he came, and the king trembled as he saw him.

Though they were at table, the tinker went into the room.

The king asked: "What did you come for at this time?"

"I came to marry your daughter."

"That life and strength may leave me if ever you get my daughter in marriage! I'd give her to death before I would to a tinker."

Now Kil Arthur, the king's son, came in, caught the tinker and hanged him, facing the front of the castle. When he was dead, they made seven parts of his body, and flung them into the sea.

Then the king had a box made so close and tight that no water could enter, and inside the box they fixed a coffin; and when they had put a bed with meat and drink into the coffin, they brought the king's daughter, laid her on the bed, closed the box, and pushed it into the open sea. The box went out with the tide and moved on the water for a long time; where it was one day it was not the next, — carried along by the waves day and night, till at last it came to another land.

Now, in the other land was a man who had spent his time in going to sea, till at length he got very poor, and said: "I'll stay at home now, since God has let me live this long. I heard my father say once that if a man would always rise early and walk along the strand, he would get his fortune from the tide at last."

One morning early, as this man was going along the strand, he saw the box, and brought it up to the shore, where he opened it and took out the coffin. When the lid was off the coffin, he found a woman inside alive.

"Oh!" said he, "I'd rather have you there than the full of the box of gold."

"I think the gold would be better for you," said the woman.

He took the stranger to his house, and gave her food and drink. Then he made a great cross on the ground, and clasping hands with the woman, jumped over the arms of the cross, going in the same direction as the sun. This was the form of marriage in that land.

They lived together pleasantly. She was a fine woman, worked well for her husband, and brought him great wealth, so that he became richer than any man; and one day, when out walking alone, he said to himself: " I am able to give a grand dinner now to Ri Fohin, Sladaire Mor [king under the wave, the great robber], who owns men, women, and every kind of beast."

Then he went home and invited Ri Fohin to dinner. He came with all the men, women, and beasts he had, and they covered the country for six miles.

The beasts were fed outside by themselves, but the people in the house. When dinner was over, he asked Ri Fohin: " Have you ever seen a house so fine and rich, or a dinner so good, as mine to-night? "

" I have not," said Ri Fohin.

Then the man went to each person present. Each gave the same answer, and said, " I have never seen such a house nor such a dinner."

He asked his wife, and she said: " My praise is no praise here; but what is this to the house and the feasting of my father, the king of Erin? "

" Why did you say that? " asked the man, and he went a second and a third time to the guests and to his wife. All had the same answers for him. Then he gave his wife a flip of the thumb on her ear, in a friendly way, and said: " Why don't you give good luck to my house; why do you give it a bad name? "

Then all the guests said: " It is a shame to strike your wife on the night of a feast."

Now the man was angry and went out of his house. It was growing dark, but he saw a champion coming on a black steed between earth and air; and the champion, who was no other than Kil Arthur, his brother-in-law, took him up and bore him away to the castle of the king of Erin.

When Kil Arthur arrived they were just sitting down to dinner in the castle, and the man dined with his father-in-law. After dinner the king of Erin had cards brought and asked his son-in-law: " Do you ever play with these? "

" No, I have never played with the like of them."

" Well, shuffle them now," said the king. He shuffled; and as they were enchanted cards and whoever held them could never lose a game he was the best player in the world, though he had never played a game before in his life.

The king said, " Put them in your pocket, they may do you good." Then the king gave him a fiddle, and asked:

" Have you ever played on the like of this? "

" Indeed I have not," said the man.

" Well, play on it now," said the king.

He played, and never in his life had he heard such music.

" Keep it," said the king; " as long as you don't let it from you, you 're the first musician on earth. Now I 'll give you something else. Here is a cup which will always give you every kind of drink you can wish for; and if all the men in the world were to drink out of it they could never empty it. Keep these three things; but never raise hand on your wife again."

The king of Erin gave him his blessing; then Kil Arthur took him up on the steed, and going between earth and sky he was soon back at his own home.

Now Ri Fohin had carried off the man's wife and all that he had while he was at dinner with the King of Erin. Going out on the road the king's son-in-law began to cry: "Oh, what shall I do; what shall I do!" and as he cried, who should come but Kil Arthur on his steed, who said, "Be quiet, I'll go for your wife and goods."

Kil Arthur went, and killed Ri Fohin and all his people and beasts, — did n't leave one alive. Then he brought back his sister to her husband, and stayed with them for three years.

One day he said to his sister: "I am going to leave you. I don't know what strength I have; I'll walk the world now till I know is there a man in it as good as myself."

Next morning he bade good-bye to his sister, and rode away on his black-haired steed, which overtook the wind before and outstripped the wind behind. He travelled swiftly till evening, spent the night in a forest, and the second day hurried on as he had the first.

The second night he spent in a forest; and next morning as he rose from the ground he saw before him a man covered with blood from fighting, and the clothes nearly torn from his body.

"What have you been doing?" asked Kil Arthur.

"I have been playing cards all night. And where are you going?" inquired the stranger of Kil Arthur.

"I am going around the world to know can I find a man as good as myself."

"Come with me," said the stranger, "and I'll show you a man who couldn't find his match till he went to fight the main ocean."

Kil Arthur went with the ragged stranger till they came to a place from which they saw a giant out on the ocean beating the waves with a club.

Kil Arthur went up to the giant's castle, and

struck the pole of combat such a blow that the giant in the ocean heard it above the noise of his club as he pounded the waves.

"What do you want?" asked the giant in the ocean, as he stopped from the pounding.

"I want you to come in here to land," said Kil Arthur, "and fight with a better man than yourself."

The giant came to land, and standing near his castle said to Kil Arthur: "Which would you rather fight with, — gray stones or sharp weapons?"

"Gray stones," said Kil Arthur.

They went at each other, and fought the most terrible battle that either of them had ever seen till that day. At last Kil Arthur pushed the giant to his shoulders through solid earth.

"Take me out of this," cried the giant, "and I'll give you my sword of light that never missed a blow, my Druidic rod of most powerful enchantment, and my healing draught which cures every sickness and wound."

"Well," said Kil Arthur, "I'll go for your sword and try it."

He went to the giant's castle for the sword, the rod, and the healing draught. When he returned the giant said: "Try the sword on that tree out there."

"Oh," said Kil Arthur, "there is no tree so good as your own neck," and with that he swept off the head of the giant; took it, and went on his way till he came to a house. He went in and put the head on a table; but that instant it disappeared, — went away of itself. Food and drink of every kind came on the table. When Kil Arthur had eaten and the table was cleared by some invisible power, the giant's head bounded on to the table, and with it a pack of cards.

"Perhaps this head wants to play with me," thought Kil Arthur, and he cut his own cards and shuffled them.

The head took up the cards and played with its mouth as well as any man could with his hands. It won all the time, — was n't playing fairly. Then Kil Arthur thought: "I'll settle this;" and he took the cards and showed how the head had taken five points in the game that did n't belong to it. Then the head sprang at him, struck and beat him till he seized and hurled it into the fire.

As soon as he had the head in the fire a beautiful woman stood before him, and said: "You have killed nine of my brothers, and this was the best of the nine. I have eight more brothers who go out to fight with four hundred men each day, and they kill them all; but next morning the four hundred are alive again and my brothers have to do battle anew. Now my mother and these eight brothers will be here soon; and they'll go down on their bended knees and curse you who killed my nine brothers, and I'm afraid your blood will rise within you when you hear the curses, and you'll kill my eight remaining brothers."

"Oh," said Kil Arthur, "I'll be deaf when the curses are spoken; I'll not hear them." Then he went to a couch and lay down. Presently the mother and eight brothers came, and cursed Kil Arthur with all the curses they knew. He heard them to the end, but gave no word from himself.

Next morning he rose early, girded on his nine-edged sword, went forth to where the eight brothers were going to fight the four hundred, and said to the eight: "Sit down, and I'll fight in your place."

Kil Arthur faced the four hundred, and fought

with them alone; and exactly at mid-day he had them all dead. "Now some one," said he, "brings these to life again. I'll lie down among them and see who it is.

Soon he saw an old hag coming with a brush in her hand, and an open vessel hanging from her neck by a string. When she came to the four hundred she dipped the brush into the vessel and sprinkled the liquid which was in it over the bodies of the men. They rose up behind her as she passed along.

"Bad luck to you," said Kil Arthur, "you are the one that keeps them alive;" then he seized her. Putting one of his feet on her two ankles, and grasping her by the head and shoulders, he twisted her body till he put the life out of her.

When dying she said: "I put you under a curse, to keep on this road till you come to the 'ram of the five rocks,' and tell him you have killed the hag of the heights and all her care."

He went to the place where the ram of the five rocks lived and struck the pole of combat before his castle. Out came the ram, and they fought till Kil Arthur seized his enemy and dashed the brains out of him against the rocks.

Then he went to the castle of the beautiful woman whose nine brothers he had killed, and for whose eight brothers he had slain the four hundred. When he appeared the mother rejoiced; the eight brothers blessed him and gave him their sister in marriage; and Kil Arthur took the beautiful woman to his father's castle in Erin, where they both lived happily and well.

SHAKING-HEAD.

THERE was once a king of a province in Erin who had an only son. The king was very careful of this son, and sent him to school for good instruction.

The other three kings of provinces in Erin had three sons at the same school; and the three sent word by this one to his father, that if he did n't put his son to death they would put both father and son to death themselves.

When the young man came home with this word to his father and mother, they were grieved when they heard it. But the king's son said that he would go out into the world to seek his fortune, and settle the trouble in that way. So away he went, taking with him only five pounds in money for his support.

The young man travelled on till he came to a grave-yard, where he saw four men fighting over a coffin. Then he went up to the four, and saw that two of them were trying to put the coffin down into a grave, and the other two preventing them and keeping the coffin above ground. When the king's son came near the men, he asked: "Why do you fight in such a place as this, and why do you keep the coffin above ground?"

Two of the men answered, and said: "The body of our brother is in this coffin, and these two men won't let us bury it."

The other two then said: "We have a debt of five pounds on the dead man, and we won't let his body be buried till the debt is paid."

The king's son said: "Do you let these men bury their brother, and I will pay what you ask."

Then the two let the brothers of the dead man bury him. The king's son paid the five pounds, and went away empty-handed, and, except the clothes on his back, he had no more than on the day he was born. After he had gone on his way awhile and the grave-yard was out of sight he turned and saw a sprightly red-haired man (*fear ruadh*) hurrying after him. When he came up, the stranger asked: "Don't you want a serving man?"

"I do not," answered the king's son, "I have nothing to support myself with, let alone a serving man."

"Well, never mind that," said the red-haired man; "I'll be with you wherever you go, whether you have anything or not."

"What is your name?" asked the king's son.

"Shaking-head," answered the red man.

When they had gone on a piece of the way together the king's son stopped and asked: "Where shall we be to-night?"

"We shall be in a giant's castle where there will be small welcome for us," said Shaking-head.

When evening came they found themselves in front of a castle. In they went and saw no one inside only a tall old hag. But they were not long in the place till they heard a loud, rushing noise outside, and a blow on the castle. The giant came; and the first words he let out of his mouth were: "I'm glad to have an Erinach on my supper-table to eat to-night." Then turning to the two he said: "What brought you here this evening; what do you want in my castle?"

"All the champions and heroes of Erin are going to take your property from you and destroy your-

self; we have come to warn you, and there is
nobody to save you from them but us," said
Shaking-head.

When the giant heard these words he changed
his treatment entirely. He gave the king's son
and Shaking-head a hearty welcome and a kindly
greeting. When he understood the news they
brought, he washed them with the tears of his
eyes, dried them with kisses, and gave them a
good supper and a soft bed that night.

Next morning the giant was up at an early hour,
and he went to the bed-side of each man and told
him to rise and have breakfast. Shaking-head
asked his reward of the giant for telling him of
the champions of Erin and the danger he was in.

"Well," said the giant, "there's a pot of gold
over there under my bed; take as much out of it
as ever you wish, and welcome."

"It isn't gold I want for my service," said Shaking-head; "you have a gift which suits me better."

"What gift is that?" asked the giant.

"The light black steed in your stable."

"That's a gift I won't give you," said the giant,
"for when any one comes to trouble or attack me,
all I have to do is to throw my leg over that steed,
and away he carries me out of sight of every
enemy."

"Well," said Shaking-head, "if you don't give
me that steed I'll bring all the kingdom of Erin
against you, and you'll be destroyed with all
you have."

The giant stopped a moment, and said: "I believe you'd do that thing, so you may take the
steed." Then Shaking-head took the steed of the
giant, gave him to the king's son, and away they
went.

At sunset Shaking-head said: "We are near

the castle of another giant, the next brother to the one who entertained us last night. He hasn't much welcome for us either; but he will treat us well when he is threatened."

The second giant was going to eat the king's son for supper, but when Shaking-head told him about the forces of Erin he changed his manner and entertained them well.

Next morning after breakfast, Shaking-head said: "You must give me a present for my services in warning you."

"There is a pot of gold under my bed," said the giant; "take all you want of it."

"I don't want your gold," said Shaking-head, "but you have a gift which suits me well."

"What is that?" asked the giant.

"The two-handed black sword that never fails a blow."

"You won't get that gift from me," said the giant; "and I can't spare it; for if a whole army were to come against me, as soon as I'd have my two hands on the hilt of that sword, I'd let no man near me without sweeping the head off him."

"Well," said Shaking-head, "I have been keeping back your enemies this long time; but I'll let them at you now, and I'll raise up more. I'll put the whole kingdom of Erin against you."

The giant stopped a moment, and said: "I believe you'd do that if it served you." So he took the sword off his belt and handed it to his guest. Shaking-head gave it to the king's son, who mounted his steed, and they both went away.

When they had gone some distance from the giant's castle Shaking-head said to the king's son, "Where shall we be to-night? — you have more knowledge than I."

" Indeed then I have not," said the king's son;
" I have no knowledge at all of where we are going; it is you who have the knowledge."

" Well," said Shaking-head, " we 'll be at the
third and youngest giant's castle to-night, and at first
he 'll treat us far worse and more harshly, but still
we 'll take this night's lodging of him, and a good
gift in the morning."

Soon after sunset they came to the castle
where they met the worst reception and the
harshest they had found on the road. The giant
was going to eat them both for supper; but when
Shaking-head told him of the champions of Erin,
he became as kind as his two brothers, and gave
good entertainment to both.

Next morning after breakfast, Shaking-head
asked for a present in return for his services.

" Do you see the pot of gold in the corner
there under my bed? — take all you want and
welcome," said the giant.

" It 's not gold I want," said Shaking-head, " but
the cloak of darkness."

" Oh," said the giant, " you 'll not get that cloak
of me, for I want it myself. If any man were to
come against me, all I 'd have to do would be to
put that cloak on my shoulders, and no one in the
world could see me, or know where I 'd be."

" Well," said Shaking-head, " it 's long enough
that I am keeping your enemies away; and if you
don't give me that cloak now I'll raise all the kingdom of Erin and still more forces to destroy you,
and it 's not long you 'll last after they come."

The giant thought a moment, and then said: " I
believe you 'd do what you say. There 's the
black cloak hanging on the wall before you;
take it."

Shaking-head took the cloak, and the two went

away together, the king's son riding on the light black steed, and having the double-handed sword at his back. When out of sight of the giant, Shaking-head put on the cloak, and was n't to be seen, and no other man could have been seen in his place. Then the king's son looked around, and began to call and search for his man, — he was lonely without him and grieved not to see him. Shaking-head, glad to see the affection of the king's son, took off the cloak and was at his side again.

"Where are we going now?" asked the king's son.

"We are going on a long journey to (Ri Chuil an Or) King Behind the Gold, to ask his daughter of him."

The two travelled on, till they came to the castle of King Behind the Gold. Then Shaking-head said: "Go in you, and ask his daughter of the king, and I 'll stay here outside with the cloak on me." So he went in and spoke to the king, and the answer he got was this: —

"I am willing to give you my daughter, but you won't get her unless you do what she will ask of you. And I must tell you now that three hundred kings' sons, lacking one, have come to ask for my daughter, and in the garden behind my castle are three hundred iron spikes, and every spike of them but one is covered with the head of a king's son who could n't do what my daughter wanted of him, and I 'm greatly in dread that your own head will be put on the one spike that is left uncovered."

"Well," said the king's son, "I 'll do my best to keep my head where it is at present."

"Stay here in my castle," said the king, "and you 'll have good entertainment till we know can you do what will be ·asked of you."

At night when the king's son was going to bed, the princess gave him a thimble, and said: "Have this for me in the morning."

He put the thimble on his finger; and she thought it could be easily taken away, if he would sleep. So she came to him in the night, with a drink, and said: "I give you this in hopes I'll gain more drink by you." He swallowed the liquor, and the princess went away with the empty cup. Then the king's son put the thimble in his mouth between his cheek and his teeth for safe keeping, and was soon asleep.

When the princess came to her own chamber, she struck her maid with a *slat an draoichta* (a rod of enchantment) and turned her into a rat; then she made such music of fifes and trumpets to sound throughout the castle, that every soul in it fell asleep. That minute, she sent the rat to where the king's son was sleeping, and the rat put her tail into the nostrils of the young man, tickled his nose so that he sneezed and blew the thimble out of his mouth. The rat caught it and ran away to the princess, who struck her with the rod of enchantment and turned her into a maid again.

Then the princess and the maid set out for the eastern world, taking the thimble with them. Shaking-head, who was watching with his cloak on, unseen by all, had seen everything, and now followed at their heels. In the eastern world, at the sea-side was a rock. The princess tapped it with her finger, and the rock opened; there was a great house inside, and in the house a giant. The princess greeted him and gave him the thimble, saying: "You're to keep this so no man can get it."

"Oh," said the giant, taking the thimble and

throwing it aside, "you need have no fear; no man can find me in this place."

Shaking-head caught the thimble from the ground and put it in his pocket. When she had finished conversation with the giant, the princess kissed him, and hurried away. Shaking-head followed her step for step, till they came at break of day to the castle of King Behind the Gold. Shaking-head went to the king's son and asked: "Was anything given you to keep last night?"

"Yes, before I came to this chamber the princess gave me her thimble, and told me to have it for her in the morning."

"Have you it now?" asked Shaking-head.

"It is not in my mouth where I put it last night, it is not in the bed; I'm afraid my head is lost," said the king's son.

"Well, look at this," said Shaking-head, taking the thimble out of his pocket and giving it to him. "The whole kingdom is moving to-day to see your death. All the people have heard that you are here asking for the princess, and they think your head 'll be put on the last spike in the garden, with the heads of the other kings' sons. Rise up now, mount your light black steed, ride to the summer-house of the princess and her father, and give her the thimble."

The king's son did as Shaking-head told him, When he gave up the thimble, the king said, "You have won one third of my daughter." But the princess was bitterly angry and vexed to the heart, that any man on earth should know that she had dealings with the giant; she cared more for that than anything else.

When the second day had passed, and the king's son was going to bed, the princess gave him a

comb to keep, and said: "If you don't have this
for me in the morning, your head will be put on
the spike that's left in my father's garden."

The king's son took the comb with him.
wrapped it in a handkerchief, and tied it to his
head.

In the night the princess came with a draught
which she gave him, and soon he was asleep.
Going back to her own chamber, she struck the
maid with her rod of enchantment, and made a
great yellow cat of her. Then she caused such music of fifes and trumpets to sound throughout the
castle that every soul was in a deep sleep before
the music was over, and that moment she sent the
cat to the chamber of the king's son. The cat
worked the handkerchief off his head, took out
the comb and ran with it to the princess, who
turned her into a maid again.

The two set out for the eastern world straightway; but if they did, Shaking-head followed them
in his cloak of darkness, till they came to the
house of the giant in the great rock at the end of
the road, at the sea. The princess gave the giant
the comb, and said: "The thimble that I gave
you to keep last night was taken from you, for the
king's son in Erin brought it back to me this morning, and has done one third of the work of winning
me, and I didn't expect you'd serve me in this
way."

When the giant heard this, he was raging, and
threw the comb into the sea behind him. Then
with Druidic spells he raised thunder and lightning and wind. The sea was roaring with storm
and rain; but the comb had not touched the water
when Shaking-head caught it.

When her talk was over the princess gave the

giant a kiss, and home she went with the maid;
but Shaking-head followed them step by step.

In the morning Shaking-head went to the king's
son, roused him, and asked: "What was your
task last night?"

"The princess gave me a comb to have for her
this morning," answered the king's son.

"Where is it now?" asked Shaking-head.

"Here on my head," said the king's son, putting up his hand to get it; but the comb was
gone. "I'm done for now," said the king's son;
"my head will be on the last spike to-day unless
I have the comb for the princess."

"Here it is for you," said Shaking-head, taking
the comb out of his pocket. "And now," said
he, "the whole kingdom is coming to this castle
to-day to see your head put on the last spike in
the garden of King Behind the Gold, for all men
think the same will happen to you that has happened to every king's son before you. Go up on
your steed and ride to the summer-house where
the king and his daughter are sitting, and give her
the comb."

The king's son did as Shaking-head bade him.
When he saw the comb the king said, "Now you
have my daughter two-thirds won." But her face
went from the princess entirely, she was so vexed
that any man should know of her dealings with
the giant.

The third night when he was going to bed the
princess said to the king's son, "If you will not
have at my father's castle to-morrow morning the
head I will kiss to-night, you'll die to-morrow, and
your own head will be put on the last spike in my
father's garden." Later in the night she came to
the bedside of the king's son with a draught, which

he drank, and before she was back in her chamber, he slept. Then she made such music all over the castle that not a soul was awake when the music had ceased. That moment she hurried away with her maid to the eastern world; but Shaking-head followed her in his cloak of darkness. This time he carried with him the two-handed sword that never failed a blow.

When she came to the rock in the eastern world and entered the house of the giant, the princess said, " You let my two gifts go with the son of the king in Erin, and he 'll have me won to-morrow if he 'll have your head at my father's castle in the morning."

" Never fear," said the giant, " there is nothing in the world to take the head off me but the double-handed sword of darkness that never fails a blow, and that sword belongs to my brother in the western world."

The princess gave the giant a kiss at parting; and as she hurried away with her maid the giant turned to look at her. His head was covered with an iron cap; but as he looked he laid bare a thin strip of his neck. Shaking-head was there near him, and said in his mind: " Your brother's sword has never been so close to your neck before; " and with one blow he swept the head off him. Then began the greatest struggle that Shaking-head ever had, to keep the head from the body of the giant. The head fought to put itself on again, and never stopped till the body was dead; then it fell to the ground. Shaking-head seized, but could n't stir the head, — could n't move it from its place. Then he searched all around it and found a (*bar an suan*) pin of slumber near the ear. When he took the pin away he had no trouble in carrying the head; and he made no delay but came to the castle at daybreak, and threw the head to a herd of pigs that belonged to the king. Then he went to the king's son, and asked:

" What happened to you last night? "

" The princess came to me, and said that if I would 'nt bring to her father's castle this morning the head she was to kiss last night, my own head would be on the last spike to-day."

" Come out with me now to the pigs," said Shaking-head.

The two went out, and Shaking-head said: " Go in among the pigs, and take the head with you to the king; and a strange head it is to put before a king."

So the king's son went on his steed to the summer-house, and gave the head to the king and his daughter, and turning to the princess, said:

" This is the head you kissed last night, and it's not a nice looking head either."

" You have my daughter won now entirely," said the king, " and she is yours. And do you take that head to the great dark hole that is out there on one side of my castle grounds, and throw it down."

The king's son mounted his steed, and rode off with the head till he came to the hole going deep into the earth. When he let down the head it went to the bottom with such a roaring and such a noise that every mare and cow and every beast in the whole kingdom cast its young, such was the terror that was caused by the noise of the head in going to the bottom of the hole.

When the head was put away the king's son went back to the castle, and married the daughter of King Behind the Gold. The wedding lasted nine days and nights, and the last night was better than the first.

When the wedding was over Shaking-head went to the king, and said: " You have provided no fortune for your daughter, and it is but right that you should remember her."

" I have plenty of gold and silver to give her," said the king.

" It is n't gold and silver that your son-in-law wants, but men to stand against his enemies, when they come on him."

" I have more treasures than men," said King Behind the Gold; " but I won't see my daughter conquered for want of an army."

They were satisfied with the king's word, and next day took the road to Erin, and kept on their way till they came opposite the grave-yard. Then Shaking-head said to the king's son: " You are no good, you have never told me a story since the first day I saw you."

" I have but one story to tell you, except what happened since we met."

" Well, tell me what happened before we met."

" I was passing this place before I saw you," said the king's son, "and four men were fighting over a coffin. I spoke to them, and two of them said they were burying the body of their brother which was in the coffin, and the others said the dead man owed them five pounds, and they would n't let the coffin into the ground until they got the money. I paid five pounds and the body was buried."

" It was my body was in the coffin," said Shaking-head, " and I came back into this world to do you a good turn; and now I am going, and you 'll never see me again unless trouble is on you."

Shaking-head disappeared, and the king's son

went home. He was n't with his father long till the other three kings' sons heard he had come back to Erin with the daughter of King Behind the Gold. They sent word, saying: "We 'll take the head off you now, and put an end to your father and yourself."

The king's son went out to walk alone, and as he was lamenting the fate he had brought on his father, who should come along to meet him but Shaking-head.

"What trouble is on you now?" asked he.

"Oh, three kings' sons are coming with their fleets and armies to destroy my father and myself, and what can we do with our one fleet and one army?"

"Well," said Shaking-head, "I 'll settle that for you without delay." Then he sent a message straight to King Behind the Gold, who gave a fleet and an army, and they came to Erin so quickly that they were at the castle before the forces of the three kings' sons. And when the three came the battle began on sea and land at both sides of the castle.

The three fleets of the three kings' sons were sunk, their armies destroyed, and the three heads taken off themselves. When the battle was over and the country safe the king resigned the castle and power to his son, and the son of a king in a province became king over all the land of Erin.

BIRTH OF FIN MACCUMHAIL.[1]

CUMHAL MACART was a great champion in the west of Erin, and it was prophesied of him that if ever he married he would meet death in the next battle he fought.

For this reason he had no wife, and knew no woman for a long time; till one day he saw the king's daughter, who was so beautiful that he forgot all fear and married her in secret.

Next day after the marriage, news came that a battle had to be fought.

Now a Druid had told the king that his daughter's son would take the kingdom from him; so he made up his mind to look after the daughter, and not let any man come near her.

Before he went to the battle, Cumhal told his mother everything, — told her of his relations with the king's daughter.

He said, "I shall be killed in battle to-day, according to the prophecy of the Druid, and I'm afraid if his daughter has a son the king will kill the child, for the prophecy is that he will lose the kingdom by the son of his own daughter. Now, if the king's daughter has a son do you hide and rear him, if you can; you will be his only hope and stay."

Cumhal was killed in the battle, and within that year the king's daughter had a son.

[1] Cumhail, genitive of Cumhal, after Mac = son; pronounced Cool.

By command of his grandfather, the boy was thrown out of the castle window into a loch, to be drowned, on the day of his birth.

The boy sank from sight; but after remaining a while under the water, he rose again to the surface, and came to land holding a live salmon in his hand.

The grandmother of the boy, Cumhal's mother, stood watching on the shore, and said to herself as she saw this: "He is my grandson, the true son of my own child," and seizing the boy, she rushed away with him, and vanished, before the king's people could stop her.

When the king heard that the old woman had escaped with his daughter's son, he fell into a terrible rage, and ordered all the male children born that day in the kingdom to be put to death, hoping in this way to kill his own grandson, and save the crown for himself.

After she had disappeared from the bank of the loch, the old woman, Cumhal's mother, made her way to a thick forest, where she spent that night as best she could. Next day she came to a great oak tree. Then she hired a man to cut out a chamber in the tree.

When all was finished, and there was a nice room in the oak for herself and her grandson, and a whelp of the same age as the boy, and which she had brought with her from the castle, she said to the man: "Give me the axe which you have in your hand, there is something here that I want to fix."

The man gave the axe into her hand, and that minute she swept the head off him, saying: "You'll never tell any man about this place now."

One day the whelp ate some of the fine chippings (*bran*) left cut by the carpenter from the inside of the tree. The old woman said: "You'll be called Bran from this out."

All three lived in the tree together, and the old woman did not take her grandson out till the end of five years; and then he could n't walk, he had been sitting so long inside.

When the old grandmother had taught the boy to walk, she brought him one day to the brow of a hill from which there was a long slope. She took a switch and said: "Now, run down this place. I will follow and strike you with this switch, and coming up I will run ahead, and you strike me as often as you can."

The first time they ran down, his grandmother struck him many times. In coming up the first time, he did not strike her at all. Every time they ran down she struck him less, and every time they ran up he struck her more.

They ran up and down for three days; and at the end of that time she could not strike him once, and he struck her at every step she took. He had now become a great runner.

When he was fifteen years of age, the old woman went with him to a hurling match between the forces of his grandfather and those of a neighboring king. Both sides were equal in skill; and neither was able to win, till the youth opposed his grandfather's people. Then, he won every game. When the ball was thrown in the air, he struck it coming down, and so again and again, — never letting the ball touch the ground till he had driven it through the barrier.

The old king, who was very angry, and greatly mortified, at the defeat of his people, exclaimed, as he saw the youth, who was very fair and had white hair: " Who is that *fin cumhal* [1] [white cap] ? "

" Ah, that is it; Fin will be his name, and Fin MacCumhail he is," said the old woman.

The king ordered his people to seize and put the young man to death, on the spot. The old woman hurried to the side of her grandson. They slipped from the crowd and away they went, a hill at a leap, a glen at a step, and thirty-two miles at a running-leap. They ran a long distance, till Fin grew tired; then the old grandmother took him on her back, putting his feet into two pockets which were in her dress, one on each side, and ran on with the same swiftness as before, a hill at a leap, a glen at a step, and thirty-two miles at a running-leap.

After a time, the old woman felt the approach of pursuit, and said to Fin: " Look behind, and tell me what you see."

" I see," said he, " a white horse with a champion on his back."

" Oh, no fear," said she; " a white horse has no endurance; he can never catch us, we are safe from him." And on they sped. A second time she felt the approach of pursuit, and again she said: " Look back, and see who is coming."

Fin looked back, and said: " I see a warrior riding on a brown horse."

" Never fear," said the old woman; "there is never a brown horse but is giddy, he cannot overtake us." She rushed on as before. A third time she said: " Look around, and see who is coming now."

---

[1] Cumhal, the name of Fin's father. Denotes also a cap or head-covering, fin = white. The punning resemblance suggested to the old woman the full name, Fin MacCumhail.

Fin looked, and said: "I see a black warrior on a black horse, following fast."

"There is no horse so tough as a black horse," said the grandmother. "There is no escape from this one. My grandson, one or both of us must die. I am old, my time has nearly come. I will die, and you and Bran save yourselves. (Bran had been with them all the time.) Right here ahead is a deep bog; you jump off my back, and escape as best you can. I'll jump into the bog up to my neck; and when the king's men come, I'll say that you are in the bog before me, sunk out of sight, and I'm trying to find you. As my hair and yours are the same color, they will think my head good enough to carry back. They will cut it off, and take it in place of yours, and show it to the king; that will satisfy his anger."

Fin slipped down, took farewell of his grandmother, and hurried on with Bran. The old woman came to the bog, jumped in, and sank to her neck. The king's men were soon at the edge of the bog, and the black rider called out to the old woman: "Where is Fin?"

"He is here in the bog before me, and I'm trying can I find him."

As the horsemen could not find Fin, and thought the old woman's head would do to carry back, they cut it off, and took it with them, saying: "This will satisfy the king."

Fin and Bran went on till they came to a great cave, in which they found a herd of goats. At the further end of the cave was a smouldering fire. The two lay down to rest.

A couple of hours later, in came a giant with a salmon in his hand. This giant was of awful height, he had but one eye, and that in the middle of his forehead, as large as the sun in heaven.

When he saw Fin, he called out: "Here, take this salmon and roast it; but be careful, for if you raise a single blister on it I'll cut the head off you. I've followed this salmon for three days and three nights without stopping, and I never let it out of my sight, for it is the most wonderful salmon in the world."

The giant lay down to sleep in the middle of the cave. Fin spitted the salmon, and held it over the fire.

The minute the giant closed the one eye in his head, he began to snore. Every time he drew breath into his body, he dragged Fin, the spit, the salmon, Bran, and all the goats to his mouth; and every time he drove a breath out of himself, he threw them back to the places they were in before. Fin was drawn time after time to the mouth of the giant with such force, that he was in dread of going down his throat.

When partly cooked, a blister rose on the salmon. Fin pressed the place with his thumb, to know could he break the blister, and hide from the giant the harm that was done. But he burned his thumb, and, to ease the pain, put it between his teeth, and gnawed the skin to the flesh, the flesh to the bone, the bone to the marrow; and when he had tasted the marrow, he received the knowledge of all things. Next moment, he was drawn by the breath of the giant right up to his face, and, knowing from his thumb what to do, he plunged the hot spit into the sleeping eye of the giant and destroyed it.

That instant the giant with a single bound was at the low entrance of the cave, and, standing with his back to the wall and a foot on each side of the opening, roared out: " You 'll not leave this place alive."

Now Fin killed the largest goat, skinned him as quickly as he could, then putting the skin on himself he drove the herd to where the giant stood; the goats passed out one by one between his legs. When the great goat came the giant took him by the horns. Fin slipped from the skin, and ran out.

" Oh, you 've escaped, " said the giant, " but before we part let me make you a present."

" I 'm afraid to go near you," said Fin; " if you wish to give me a present, put it out this way, and then go back."

The giant placed a ring on the ground, then went back. Fin took up the ring and put it on the end of his little finger above the first joint. It clung so firmly that no man in the world could have taken it off.

The giant then called out, " Where are you? "

" On Fin's finger, " cried the ring. That instant the giant sprang at Fin and almost came down on his head, thinking in this way to crush him to bits. Fin sprang to a distance. Again the giant asked, " Where are you? "

" On Fin's finger," answered the ring.

Again the giant made a leap, coming down just in front of Fin. Many times he called and many times almost caught Fin, who could not escape with the ring on his finger. While in this terrible struggle, not knowing how to escape, Bran ran up and asked:

" Why don't you chew your thumb? "

Fin bit his thumb to the marrow, and then knew what to do. He took the knife with which he had skinned the goat, cut off his finger at the first joint, and threw it, with the ring still on, into a deep bog near by.

Again the giant called out, "Where are you?" and the ring answered, "On Fin's finger."

Straightway the giant sprang towards the voice, sank to his shoulders in the bog, and stayed there.

Fin with Bran now went on his way, and travelled till he reached a deep and thick wood, where a thousand horses were drawing timber, and men felling and preparing it.

"What is this?" asked Fin of the overseer of the workmen.

"Oh, we are building a dun (a castle) for the king; we build one every day, and every night it is burned to the ground. Our king has an only daughter; he will give her to any man who will save the dun, and he'll leave him the kingdom at his death. If any man undertakes to save the dun and fails, his life must pay for it; the king will cut his head off. The best champions in Erin have tried and failed; they are now in the king's dungeons, a whole army of them, waiting the king's pleasure. He's going to cut the heads off them all in one day."

"Why don't you chew your thumb?" asked Bran.

Fin chewed his thumb to the marrow, and then knew that on the eastern side of the world there lived an old hag with her three sons, and every evening at nightfall she sent the youngest of these to burn the king's dun.

"I will save the king's dun," said Fin.

"Well," said the overseer, "better men than you have tried and lost their lives."

"Oh," said Fin, "I'm not afraid; I'll try for the sake of the king's daughter."

Now Fin, followed by Bran, went with the overseer to the king. "I hear you will give your daughter to the man who saves your dun," said Fin.

"I will," said the king; "but if he fails I must have his head."

"Well," said Fin, "I'll risk my head for the sake of your daughter. If I fail I'm satisfied." The king gave Fin food and drink; he supped, and after supper went to the dun.

"Why don't you chew your thumb?" said Bran; "then you'll know what to do." He did. Then Bran took her place on the roof, waiting for the old woman's son. Now the old woman in the east told her youngest · son to hurry on with his torches, burn the dun, and come back without delay; for the stirabout was boiling and he must not be too late for supper.

He took the torches, and shot off through the air with a wonderful speed. Soon he was in sight of the king's dun, threw the torches upon the thatched roof to set it on fire as usual.

That moment Bran gave the torches such a push with her shoulders, that they fell into the stream which ran around the dun, and were put out. "Who is this," cried the youngest son of the old hag, "who has dared to put out my lights, and interfere with my hereditary right?"

"I," said Fin, who stood in front of him. Then began a terrible battle between Fin and the old woman's son. Bran came down from the dun to help Fin; she bit and tore his enemy's back, stripping the skin and flesh from his head to his heels.

After a terrible struggle such as had not been in

the world before that night, Fin cut the head off his enemy. But for Bran, Fin could never have conquered.

The time for the return of her son had passed; supper was ready. The old woman, impatient and angry, said to the second son: "You take torches and hurry on, see why your brother loiters. I'll pay him for this when he comes home! But be careful and don't do like him, or you'll have your pay too. Hurry back, for the stirabout is boiling and ready for supper."

He started off, was met and killed exactly as his brother, except that he was stronger and the battle fiercer. But for Bran, Fin would have lost his life that night.

The old woman was raging at the delay, and said to her eldest son, who had not been out of the house for years: (It was only in case of the greatest need that she sent him. He had a cat's head, and was called Pus an Chuine, "Puss of the Corner;" he was the eldest and strongest of all the brothers.) "Now take torches, go and see what delays your brothers; I'll pay them for this when they come home."

The eldest brother shot off through the air, came to the king's dun, and threw his torches upon the roof. They had just singed the straw a little, when Bran pushed them off with such force that they fell into the stream and were quenched.

"Who is this," screamed Cat-head, "who dares to interfere with my ancestral right?"

"I," shouted Fin. Then the struggle began fiercer than with the second brother. Bran helped from behind, tearing the flesh from his head to his heels; but at length Cat-head fastened his teeth into Fin's breast, biting and gnawing till Fin cut the head off. The body fell to the ground, but the head lived, gnawing as terribly as before. Do what they could it was impossible to kill it. Fin hacked and cut, but could neither kill nor pull it off. When nearly exhausted, Bran said:

" Why don't you chew your thumb? "

Fin chewed his thumb, and reaching the marrow knew that the old woman in the east was ready to start with torches to find her sons, and burn the dun herself, and that she had a vial of liquid with which she could bring the sons to life; and that nothing could free him from Cat-head but the old woman's blood.

After midnight the old hag, enraged at the delay of her sons, started and shot through the air like lightning, more swiftly than her sons. She threw her torches from afar upon the roof of the dun; but Bran as before hurled them into the stream.

Now the old woman circled around in the air looking for her sons. Fin was getting very weak from pain and loss of blood, for Cat-head was biting at his breast all the time.

Bran called out: " Rouse yourself, oh, Fin; use all your power or we are lost! If the old hag gets a drop from the vial upon the bodies of her sons, they will come to life, and then we're done for."

Thus roused, Fin with one spring reached the old woman in the air, and swept the bottle from her grasp; which falling upon the ground was emptied.

The old hag gave a scream which was heard all over the world, came to the ground and closed with Fin. Then followed a battle greater than the world had ever known before that night, or has ever seen since. Water sprang out of gray rocks, cows cast their calves even when they had none, and hard rushes grew soft in the remotest corner of Erin, so desperate was the fighting and so awful, between Fin and the old hag. Fin would have died that night but for Bran.

Just as daylight was coming Fin swept the head off the old woman, caught some of her blood, and rubbed it around Cat-head, who fell off dead.

He rubbed his own wounds with the blood and was cured; then rubbed some on Bran, who had been singed with the torches, and she was as well as ever. Fin, exhausted with fighting, dropped down and fell asleep.

While he was sleeping the chief steward of the king came to the dun, found it standing safe and sound, and seeing Fin lying there asleep knew that he had saved it. Bran tried to waken Fin, pulled and tugged, but could not rouse him.

The steward went to the king, and said: "I have saved the dun, and I claim the reward."

"It shall be given you," answered the king; and straightway the steward was recognized as the king's son-in-law, and orders were given to make ready for the wedding.

Bran had listened to what was going on, and when her master woke, exactly at midday, she told him of all that was taking place in the castle of the king.

Fin went to the king, and said: "I have saved your dun, and I claim the reward."

"Oh," said the king, "my steward claimed the reward, and it has been given to him."

"He had nothing to do with saving the dun; I saved it," said Fin.

"Well," answered the king, "he is the first man who told me of its safety and claimed the reward."

" Bring him here : let me look at him," said Fin.

He was sent for, and came. " Did you save the king's dun ? " asked Fin. " I did," said the steward.

" You did not, and take that for your lies," said Fin; and striking him with the edge of his open hand he swept the head off his body, dashing it against the other side of the room, flattening it like paste on the wall.

" You are the man," said the king to Fin, " who saved the dun; yours is the reward. All the champions, and there is many a man of them, who have failed to save it are in the dungeons of my fortress; their heads must be cut off before the wedding takes place."

" Will you let me see them ? " asked Fin.

" I will," said the king.

Fin went down to the men, and found the first champions of Erin in the dungeons. " Will you obey me in all things if I save you from death?" said Fin. " We will," said they. Then he went back to the king and asked:

" Will you give me the lives of these champions of Erin, in place of your daughter's hand ? "

" I will," said the king.

All the champions were liberated, and left the king's castle that day. Ever after they followed the orders of Fin, and these were the beginning of his forces and the first of the Fenians of Erin.

FIN MACCUMHAIL AND THE FENIANS OF ERIN IN THE CASTLE OF FEAR DUBH.

IT was the custom with Fin MacCumhail and the Fenians of Erin, when a stranger from any part of the world came to their castle, not to ask him a question for a year and a day.

On a time, a champion came to Fin and his men, and remained with them. He was not at all pleasant or agreeable.

At last Fin and his men took counsel together; they were much annoyed because their guest was so dull and morose, never saying a word, always silent.

While discussing what kind of man he was, Diarmuid Duivne offered to try him; so one evening when they were eating together, Diarmuid came and snatched from his mouth the hind-quarter of a bullock, which he was picking.

Diarmuid pulled at one part of the quarter, — pulled with all his strength, but only took the part that he seized, while the other kept the part he held. All laughed; the stranger laughed too, as heartily as any. It was the first laugh they had heard from him.

The strange champion saw all their feats of arms and practised with them, till the year and a day were over. Then he said to Fin and his men:

"I have spent a pleasant year in your company; you gave me good treatment, and the least

I can do now is to give you a feast at my own castle."

No one had asked what his name was up to that time. Fin now asked his name. He answered: " My name is Fear Dubh, of Alba."

Fin accepted the invitation; and they appointed the day for the feast, which was to be in Erin, since Fear Dubh did not wish to trouble them to go to Alban. He took leave of his host and started for home.

When the day for the feast came, Fin and the chief men of the Fenians of Erin set out for the castle of Fear Dubh.

They went, a glen at a step, a hill at a leap, and thirty-two miles at a running leap, till they came to the grand castle where the feast was to be given.

They went in; everything was ready, seats at the table, and every man's name at his seat in the same order as at Fin's castle. Diarmuid, who was always very sportive, — fond of hunting, and paying court to women, was not with them; he had gone to the mountains with his dogs.

All sat down, except Conan Maol MacMorna (never a man spoke well of him); no seat was ready for him, for he used to lie on the flat of his back on the floor, at Fin's castle.

When all were seated the door of the castle closed of itself. Fin then asked the man nearest the door, to rise and open it. The man tried to rise; he pulled this way and that, over and hither, but he could n't get up. Then the next man tried, and the next, and so on, till the turn came to Fin himself, who tried in vain.

Now, whenever Fin and his men were in trouble and great danger it was their custom to raise a cry of distress (a voice of howling), heard all over Erin.   Then all men knew that they were in peril of death; for they never raised this cry except in the last extremity.

Fin's son, Fialan, who was three years old and in the cradle, heard the cry, was roused, and jumped up.

"Get me a sword!" said he to the nurse. "My father and his men are in distress; I must go to aid them."

"What could you do, poor little child."

Fialan looked around, saw an old rusty sword-blade laid aside for ages. He took it down, gave it a snap; it sprang up so as to hit his arm, and all the rust dropped off; the blade was pure as shining silver.

"This will do," said he; and then he set out towards the place where he heard the cry, going a glen at a step, a hill at a leap, and thirty-two miles at a running leap, till he came to the door of the castle, and cried out.

Fin answered from inside, "Is that you, my child?"

"It is," said Fialan.

"Why did you come?"

"I heard your cry, and how could I stay at home, hearing the cry of my father and the Fenians of Erin!"

"Oh, my child, you cannot help us much."

Fialan struck the door powerfully with his sword, but no use. Then, one of the men inside asked Fin to chew his thumb, to know what was keeping them in, and why they were bound.

Fin chewed his thumb, from skin to blood, from blood to bone, from bone to marrow, and discovered that Fear Dubh had built the castle by magic, and that he was coming himself with a great force to cut the head off each one of them. (These men from Alba had always a grudge against the champions of Erin.)

Said Fin to Fialan: "Do you go now, and stand at the ford near the castle, and meet Fear Dubh."

Fialan went and stood in the middle of the ford. He was n't long there when he saw Fear Dubh coming with a great army.

"Leave the ford, my child," said Fear Dubh, who knew him at once. "I have not come to harm your father. I spent a pleasant year at his castle. I've only come to show him honor."

"I know why you have come," answered Fialan. "You 've come to destroy my father and all his men, and I 'll not leave this ford while I can hold it."

"Leave the ford; I don't want to harm your father, I want to do him honor. If you don't let us pass my men will kill you," said Fear Dubh.

"I will not let you pass so long as I 'm alive before you," said Fialan.

The men faced him; and if they did Fialan kept his place, and a battle commenced, the like of which was never seen before that day. Fialan went through the army as a hawk through a flock of sparrows on a March morning, till he killed every man except Fear Dubh. Fear Dubh told him again to leave the ford, he didn't want to harm his father.

"Oh!" said Fialan, "I know well what you want."

"If you don't leave that place I 'll make you leave it!" said Fear Dubh. Then they closed in combat; and such a combat was never seen before between any two warriors. They made springs to rise through the centre of hard gray rocks, cows to cast their calves whether they had them or not. All the horses of the country were racing about and neighing in dread and fear, and all created things were terrified at the sound and clamor of the fight, till the weapons of Fear Dubh went to pieces in the struggle, and Fialan made two halves of his own sword.

Now they closed in wrestling. In the first round Fialan put Fear Dubh to his knees in the hard bottom of the river; the second round he put him to his hips, and the third, to his shoulders.

"Now," said he, "I have you," giving him a stroke of the half of his sword, which cut the head off him.

Then Fialan went to the door of the castle and told his father what he had done.

Fin chewed his thumb again, and knew what other danger was coming. "My son," said he to Fialan, "Fear Dubh has a younger brother more powerful than he was; that brother is coming against us now with greater forces than those which you have destroyed."

As soon as Fialan heard these words he hurried to the ford, and waited till the second army came up. He destroyed this army as he had the other, and closed with the second brother in a fight fiercer and more terrible than the first; but at last he thrust him to his armpits in the hard bottom of the river and cut off his head.

Then he went to the castle, and told his father what he had done. A third time Fin chewed his thumb, and said: "My son, a third army more to be dreaded than the other two is coming now to destroy us, and at the head of it is the youngest brother of Fear Dubh, the most desperate and powerful of the three."

Again Fialan rushed off to the ford; and, though the work was greater than before, he left not a man of the army alive. Then he closed with the youngest brother of Fear Dubh, and if the first and second battles were terrible this was more terrible by far; but at last he planted the youngest brother up to his armpits in the hard bottom of the river, and swept the head off him.

Now, after the heat and struggle of combat Fialan was in such a rage that he lost his mind from fury, not having any one to fight against; and if the whole world had been there before him he would have gone through it and conquered it all.

But having no one to face him he rushed along the river-bank, tearing the flesh from his own body. Never had such madness been seen in any created being before that day.

Diarmuid came now and knocked at the door of the castle, having the dog Bran with him, and asked Fin what had caused him to raise the cry of distress.

" Oh, Diarmuid," said Fin, " we are all fastened in here to be killed. Fialan has destroyed three armies, and Fear Dubh with his two brothers. He is raging now along the bank of the river; you must not go near him, for he would tear you limb from limb. At this moment he would n't spare me, his own father; but after a while he will cease from raging and die down; then you can go. The mother of Fear Dubh is coming, and will soon be at the ford. She is more violent, more venomous, more to be dreaded, a greater warrior than her sons. The chief weapon she has are the nails on her fingers; each nail is seven perches long, of the hardest steel on earth. She is coming in the air at this moment with the speed of a hawk, and she has a kŭ́ran (a small vessel), with liquor in it, which has such power that if she puts three drops of it on the mouths of her sons they will rise up as well as ever; and if she brings them to life there is nothing to save us.

" Go to the ford; she will be hovering over the corpses of the three armies to know can she find her sons, and as soon as she sees them she will dart down and give them the liquor. You must rise with a mighty bound upon her, dash the kŭ́ran out of her hand and spill the liquor.

" If you can kill her save her blood, for nothing in the world can free us from this place and open the door of the castle but the blood of the old hag. I'm in dread you'll not succeed, for she is far more terrible than all her sons together. Go now; Fialan is dying away, and the old woman is coming; make no delay."

Diarmuid hurried to the ford, stood watching a while; then he saw high in the air something no larger than a hawk. As it came nearer and nearer he saw it was the old woman. She hovered high in the air over the ford. At last she saw her sons, and was swooping down, when Diarmuid rose with a bound into the air and struck the vial a league out of her hand.

The old hag gave a shriek that was heard to the eastern world, and screamed: " Who has dared to interfere with me or my sons? "

" I," answered Diarmuid; " and you'll not go further till I do to you what has been done to your sons."

The fight began; and if there ever was a fight, before or since, it could not be more terrible than this one; but great as was the power of Diarmuid he never could have conquered but for Bran the dog.

The old woman with her nails stripped the skin and flesh from Diarmuid almost to the vitals. But Bran tore the skin and flesh off the old woman's back from her head to her heels.

From the dint of blood-loss and fighting, Diarmuid was growing faint. Despair came on him, and he was on the point of giving way, when a little robin flew near to him, and sitting on a bush, spoke, saying:

" Oh, Diarmuid, take strength; rise and sweep the head off the old hag, or Fin and the Fenians of Erin are no more."

Diarmuid took courage, and with his last strength made one great effort, swept the head off the old hag and caught her blood in a vessel. He rubbed some on his own wounds, — they were cured; then he cured Bran.

Straightway he took the blood to the castle, rubbed drops of it on the door, which opened, and he went in.

All laughed with joy at the rescue. He freed Fin and his men by rubbing the blood on the chairs; but when he came as far as Conan Maol the blood gave out.

All were going away. " Why should you leave me here after you; " cried Conan Maol, " I would rather die at once than stay here for a lingering death. Why don't you, Oscar, and you, Gol Mac-Morna, come and tear me out of this place; anyhow you'll be able to drag the arms out of me and kill me at once; better that than leave me to die alone."

Oscar and Gol took each a hand, braced their

feet against his feet, put forth all their strength and brought him standing; but if they did, he left all the skin and much of the flesh from the back of his head to his heels on the floor behind him.   He was covered with blood, and by all accounts was in a terrible condition, bleeding and wounded.

Now there were sheep grazing near the castle. The Fenians ran out, killed and skinned the largest and best of the flock, and clapped the fresh skin on Conan's back; and such was the healing power in the sheep, and the wound very fresh, that Conan's back healed, and he marched home with the rest of the men, and soon got well; and if he did, they sheared off his back wool enough every year to make a pair of stockings for each one of the Fenians of Erin, and for Fin himself.

And that was a great thing to do and useful, for wool was scarce in Erin in those days.   Fin and his men lived pleasantly and joyously for some time; and if they did n't, may we.

FIN MACCUMHAIL AND THE KNIGHT OF THE FULL AXE.

THERE was a day when Fin went on an expedition by himself. He walked out to his currochán on the seashore, gave it a kick that sent it out nine leagues from land, then with a spring he jumped into the boat and rowed over the sea.

After he had gone some distance he saw a giant coming towards him, walking through the water, which did not reach his knees. Looking up, Fin could see nothing between the head of the giant and the sky.

With one step the giant was in front of Fin, and it seemed that he and his boat would be lost in a moment between the legs of the terrible monster.

"Poor, little helpless creature! what brings you here in my way?" asked the giant. He was just going to lay hold of the boat and toss it far off to one side, when Fin called out:

"Won't you give fair play; just let me put foot on solid land, and see what will happen. Don't attack me here; I'm not afraid to meet you once I have earth for my two feet to stand on."

"If that is all you want I can take you to land very soon." And seizing the boat as he would a grass-blade, the giant drew it to the shore of the sea opposite to that from which Fin started, and in front of his own castle.

"What will you do now?" asked the giant.

"I'll fight with you," said Fin.

The giant brought out his battle-axe, which had a blade seven acres in size. Fin was ready with his sword, and now began a most terrible battle.

Fin faced the giant, slashing at him with his sword, and when the giant made an offer of the axe at him, Fin would dart to one side; and when the axe missing him struck the ground, it went into the handle. The giant was a long time striving to know could he draw out the axe; and while at this Fin ran behind and cut steps with his sword into the leg of his enemy; and by the time the giant had the axe out of the ground, Fin was ready for him again and in front of him, striking and vexing him with his sword. It was another long while till a blow came down; and when the axe went into the ground again, Fin ran behind a second time, cut more steps in the leg and body of the giant, so as to reach his neck and cut the head off him.

When the axe was coming to the ground the third time, Fin slipped and fell under one corner of it, and between the feet of the giant, who closed his legs with a clap that was heard to the end of the Western World. He thought to catch Fin; but Fin was too quick for him, and though badly hurt he was able to cut more steps and climb to the neck of the giant. With one blow he swept the head off him, — and a big head it was; by all accounts as broad as the moon.

The battle was fought in front of the giant's castle. Fin was terribly wounded; the axe had cut that deep that his bowels were to be seen. He dropped at the side of the giant, and lay helpless on the ground.

After the fall of the giant twelve women came out of his castle, and when they drew near and saw him dead they laughed from joy; but seeing Fin with his wound they began to mourn.

"Oh, then," said Fin, "is it making sport of me you are after the evil day that I've had?"

"Indeed it is not. We are twelve daughters of kings, stolen from our fathers. We saw the giant fall, and came here to look at him dead; we grieve for you and mourn for the sorrow that is on you, but we are so glad the giant is killed that we cannot help laughing."

"Well," said Fin, "if you mourn for me and are glad that I have killed the giant, will you carry me to my currochán, lay me in it, and push it out to sea? The waves may bear me home, and I care for nothing else if only one day my bones may come to land in Erin."

The twelve women took him up carefully and put him in the boat, and when the tide came they pushed it out to sea.

Fin lay in the bottom of the boat barely alive. It floated along, and he was borne over the waves. Hither and thither went the boat, till at last one day a blackbird came down on the body of Fin MacCumhail, and began to pick at his entrails. The blackbird said:

"Many a long day have I watched and waited for this chance, and glad am I to have it now."

That moment the blackbird turned into a little man not more than three feet high. Then he said: "I was under a Druidic spell, to be a blackbird till I should get three bites of fat from the entrails of Fin MacCumhail. I have followed you everywhere; have watched you in battle and hunt, on sea and land, but never have I been able to get the chance till this day. Now I have it, I have also the power to make you well again."

He put Fin's entrails into their proper place, rubbed him with an ointment that he had, and Fin was well as ever.

The little man, who said his name was Ridiri na lan tur (Knight of the Full Axe) had a small axe, his only weapon. As they floated along he said to Fin: " I wish to show you some strange things, such as you have never seen in Erin. We are near a country where the king's daughter is to be married to-night. We will prevent the ceremony."

" Oh no," said Fin, " I would rather go to my own home."

" Never mind," said the little man, " nothing can harm you in my company; come with me. This is a wonderful king, and he has a wonderful daughter. It's a strange country, and I want to show you the place. We 'll tell him that you are Fin MacCumhail, monarch of Erin; that we have been shipwrecked, and ask for a night's shelter."

Fin consented at last, and with the Knight of the Full Axe landed, drew the boat on shore, and went to the king's castle. There was noise and tumult; great crowds of people had come to do honor to the king's daughter. Never before had such preparations been made in that kingdom.

The Knight of the Full Axe knocked at the door, and asked admission for himself and Fin MacCumhail, monarch of Erin, shipwrecked on that shore. (The country was north of Erin, far out in the sea.)

The attendants said: " No strangers may enter here, but there is a great house further on; go there and welcome."

The house to which they were directed was

twenty-one miles long, ten miles wide, and about
five miles distant from the castle; inhabited by the
strangest men in the world, body-guards of the king,
fed from the king's house, and a terrible feeding it
was, — human flesh. All strangers who came to
the king's castle were sent to that house, where the
guards tore them to pieces and ate them up.

These guards had to be fed well; if not they
would devour the whole country.

With Fin and the Knight of the Full Axe there
went a messenger, who was careful not to go near
the house; he pointed it out from a distance, and
ran home.

Fin and the knight knocked at the door. When
it was opened all inside laughed; as they laughed,
Fin could see their hearts and livers they were so
glad. The Knight of the Full Axe asked, " Why
do you laugh in this way? "

" Oh," answered they, " we laugh because you
are so small you 'll not make a mouthful for one
of us."

The guards barred the door and put a prop
against it. Now the knight put a second prop
against the door; the guards asked, " Why do you
do that? "

" I do it so none of you may escape me," answered the knight. Then seizing two of the
largest of the guards, one in each hand, he used
them as clubs and killed the others with them.
He ran the length of the house, striking right and
left, till he walloped the life out of all that was in
it, but the two. To them he said: " I spare you
to clean out the house, and make the place fit
for the monarch of Erin to spend the night in.
Bring rushes, and make ready to receive Fin
MacCumhail."

And from wherever they got them, they brought

two baskets of rushes, each basket as big as a mountain, and spread litter on the ground two feet deep through the whole house; and then at the knight's command they brought a pile of turf, and made a grand fire.

Late in the evening the king's attendants brought food, which they left near the house of the guards; these monsters were fed twice a day, morning and evening. To their great surprise the attendants saw the bodies of the dead giants piled up outside the house; they ran off quickly to tell the news.

Now the Knight of the Full Axe sat by the fire. The two guards that he had spared tried to chat and be agreeable; but the knight snapped at them and said: "What company are you for the monarch of Erin?" Then he caught the two, squeezed the life out of them, and threw them on the pile outside.

"Now," said the knight to Fin, "there is no suitable food for you; I must get you something good to eat from the castle."

So off he started, reached the castle quickly, knocked at the door, and demanded the best of food, saying, "'T is fine treatment you are giving the monarch of Erin to-night!"

They trembled at the voice of the little man, and without words or delay gave him the best they had in the castle. He carried it back and placed it before Fin. "Now," said he, "they have given us no wine; we must have wine, and that of the best."

"Oh, we have no need of wine!" said Fin; but off went the knight.

Again he demanded supplies at the castle. He took a hogshead of the best wine, threw it over his shoulder, and, as he hurried out, he struck a jamb off the door and swept it along with the hogshead.

"Now," said the knight, after they had eaten and drunk, "'t is too bad for the monarch of Erin to sleep on rushes; he should have the best bed in the land."

"Oh, trouble yourself no further," said Fin; "better sleep on rushes than all this noise."

But the knight would listen to nothing; away he went to the castle, and shouted: "Give me the best bed in this place! I want it for Fin Mac-Cumhail, the monarch of Erin."

They gave him the bed in a moment. With hurried steps he was back, and said to Fin: "Rest on this bed. Now I'll stop the wedding of the princess; you may take her to Erin if you like."

"Oh, that would not be right! I am well as I am," said Fin, who was getting in dread of the knight himself.

"No, you'd better have the princess," and off rushed the knight. He entered the castle. All were in terror; hither and thither they hurried, not knowing what to do. The Knight of the Full Axe seized the princess. "The monarch of Erin is a better man than your bridegroom," said he; and clapping her under his arm, away he went. Not a man had the courage to stir.

All was confusion and fear in the king's castle. The princess was gone and no one could save her. All were in terrible dread, knowing what had been done at the long house.

At last an old hag, one of the queen's waiting-women, said: "I'll go and see what has become of the princess. I'll go on the chimney and look down."

Off ran the hag, and never rested till she was on

the top of the chimney, sticking down her head to know what could she see. The chimney was wide, for the king's guards had cooked all their food below on the fire. The Knight of the Full Axe was looking up at the time and saw the two eyes staring down at him.

" Go on out of that," cried he, flinging his axe; which stuck in the old woman's forehead. Off she rushed to the castle. She had seen nothing of the princess; all she knew was that a little man was sitting by the fire warming himself, that he had thrown his axe at her, and it had stuck in her forehead.

At daylight the knight spoke to Fin, who rose at once. "Now," said he, "I have no strength left; all my strength is in the axe. While I had that I could do anything, now I can do nothing. We are in great danger; but there is such dread of us on the people here that we may mend matters yet. Do you put on the dress of a leech, get herbs and vials, and pretend you have great skill in healing. Go to the castle, and say you can take the axe out of the old hag's head. No man there can do that without killing her; she will die the minute it is drawn. Get at her, seize the axe, pull it out, and with it you will have the greatest power on earth."

Fin went to the castle, and said: " I am a great doctor. I can take the axe out of the old woman's head without trouble."

They took him to the hag, who was sitting upright in bed; her head was so sore she could n't lie down. He felt her head around the axe, sent the people away; when they were gone he took hold of the handle. With one snap he made two halves of the old woman's head.

Fin ran out with the axe, leaving the old hag dead behind him. He never stopped till he came where he had left the knight.

Fin MacCumhail was now the strongest man on earth, and the knight the weakest. "You may keep the axe," said the little man; "I shall not envy you, but will go with you and you will protect me."

"No," said Fin, "it shall never be said that I took the axe from you, though I know its value and feel its power."

The knight was glad to get back his axe, and now the two set out for Erin. Fin kicked the boat three leagues from land, and with a bound they both came down in it, and floated on till they saw the coast of Erin. Then the little man said:

"I must leave you now. Though of your kin, I cannot land in Erin. But if you need me at any time you have only to look over your right shoulder, call my name, and you will see me before you."

Now Fin sprang ashore; he had been absent a year and more, and no man knew where he was while gone. All thought him lost. Great was the gladness when Fin came home, and told the Fenians of Erin of what he had seen and what he had done.

GILLA NA GRAKIN AND FIN MAC-CUMHAIL.

THERE was a blacksmith in Dun Kinealy beyond Killybegs, and he had two young men serving him whose names were Césa MacRi na Tulach and Lun Dubh MacSmola.

When their time was up the young men settled with the blacksmith and took their pay of him. After they had eaten breakfast in the morning they went away together.

When they had gone some distance from the house they changed their gait, so that when they took one step forward they took two backwards; and when evening came they were not five perches away from the house where they had eaten breakfast in the morning.

Then one said to the other: "I suppose what is on one of us is on the other."

"What's that?" asked the first.

"We are both in love with Scéhide ni Wánanan."

"That is true," said the other, "we are both in love with the blacksmith's maid."

When this was said they turned and went back to the house. The blacksmith welcomed them, and was glad.

"You need not welcome us," said they; "we have not come back to you to seek hire; but we are both in love with Scéhide ni Wánanan, and you 'll have to settle the matter for us."

"Well," said the blacksmith, "I can do that.

We 'll open the two doors of the forge, and let you and the maiden go in and stand in the middle of the place. Then do you two go out, one at each door, and the man she 'll follow will have her."

The three came in, — one man went out at each door of the forge; Scéhide followed Lun Dubh.

When he saw this Césa spoke up, and said: " I 'm willing to leave her with you; but turn back a moment here to me, for the word that 'll be between us."

Lun Dubh turned back into the forge, and Césa said: " Put your finger on this anvil."

Lun Dubh put his finger on the anvil. Césa, catching up a good spike, which the old blacksmith had made, and a hammer drove the spike through the finger of Lun Dubh, fastening him to the anvil.

" Now," said Lun Dubh to Césa; " let me go free, and do you take Scéhide; but I must have the first blow on you in battle or war, or wherever else I meet you in the world."

" I will give you that," said Césa. So he freed his comrade from the anvil. The young men parted from each other, — Lun Dubh went one way alone, ánd Césa another with Scéhide ni Wánanan.

As Césa went along he bought a skin at every house where he could find one, until he had enough to make clothes in which to disguise himself; for he was in dread of Lun Dubh, on account of the first blow which he had the right to strike when they met.

He put on the skin clothes, and changed his name to Gilla na Grakin (the fellow of the skins).

Gilla and his wife held on their way till they came to the castle of Fin MacCumhail; and the time they came there was no one in the place but women.

"Where is Fin MacCumhail with his men to-day?" asked Gilla na Grakin.

"They are all out hunting," said the women.

Now Gilla saw that the castle stood with open door facing the wind, and turning again to the women he asked: "Why do you have the door of the castle to the wind?"

"When Fin and his men are at home and the wind comes in at the door, they all go out, take hold of the castle and turn it around till the door is on the sheltered side."

When Gilla na Grakin heard this he went out, put his hands to the castle, and turned it around till the door was on the sheltered side.

In the evening when Fin and the Fenians of Erin were coming from the hunt, they saw the castle turned around, and Fin said to the men: "I'm afraid we have n't half enough of game for the supper of the strangers who have come to visit us to-day, there are so many of them that they have turned the castle around."

When they came home they saw there was no man there but Gilla na Grakin, and they wondered at the work he had done.

Gilla stood before Fin, and said: "Do you want a serving man?"

"I do indeed," said Fin.

"What wages will you give me for a year and a day?" asked Gilla.

"What yourself will ask," replied Fin.

"I wont ask much," said Gilla; "five pounds for myself, and a room in the castle for my wife."

"You shall have both," said Fin.

"I'm your man now," said Gilla.

The whole company spent the first part of that night in ease, the second in sport, and the third in a short sleep.

The next morning all the Fenians of Erin were going to hunt, as the day before, and Fin said to Gilla na Grakin: "Will you take any man to help you?"

"I'll take no man with me but myself; and do you let me go in one part of the country alone, and go yourself with all your men in another part."

"Well," said Fin," will you find dry glens of ridges, or go in deep boggy places where there is danger of drowning?"

"I will go in deep boggy places."

All left the castle to hunt. Fin and the Fenians of Erin went in one direction, and Gilla na Grakin in another, and hunted all day.

When they came home in the evening Gilla na Grakin had a thousand times more game than Fin and all his men together.

When Fin saw this he was glad to have such a good man, and was pleased beyond measure with Gilla na Grakin. The whole company spent that night as they had the night before, — in ease and sport and sleep.

Next day Conan Maol was outside with Fin, and he said: "Gilla na Grakin will destroy the Fenians of Erin and put you and all of us to death, unless you banish him in some way from this castle."

"Well;" said Fin to Conan Maol, "I've never had a good man but you wanted me to put him away. And how could I banish such a man as this if I tried?"

"The way to banish him," said Conan Maol, "is to send him to the king of Lochlin to take from him the pot of plenty that's never without meat, but has always enough in it to feed the whole world, and bring that pot to this castle."

Fin called Gilla na Grakin, and said: "You'll have to go for me now to the king of Lochlin, and get from him the pot of plenty that is never without meat, and bring it here to me."

"Well," said Gilla, " as long as I'm in your service I can't refuse to do your work."

So away went Gilla. He took a glen at a step and a hill at a leap till he came to the shore of the sea, where he caught up two sticks, put one across the other, then gave them a tip of the hand, and a fine vessel rose out of the two pieces of wood.

Gilla na Grakin went on board the vessel, hoisted the sails, and off he went in a straight line. The music he heard on his way was the whistling of eels in the sea and the calling of gulls in the air, till he came under the king's castle in Lochlin. When he came, there were hundreds of ships standing near the shore, and he had to anchor outside them all; then he stepped from ship to ship till he stood on land.

What should there be at the time he landed but a great feast in the castle of the king. So Gilla went to the front of the castle and stood outside at the door; but he could go no further for the crowd, and no one looked at him. At last he shouted: " This is a very hospitable feast, and you are a people of fine manners not to ask a stranger is he hungry or thirsty."

"You are right," said the king, who turned to the people and said: " Give the pot of plenty to the stranger till he eats his fill."

The people obeyed the king, and when Gilla na Grakin got hold of the pot he made for the ship, and never stopped till he was on board. He put

the pot in a safe place below. Then standing on
deck he said to himself: " It is no use to take
the pot by my swiftness unless I take it by my
strength."

So he turned and went to land again. All the
heroes and champions of the king of Lochlin and
his whole army were ready to fight, but if they
were so was Gilla na Grakin.

When he came up to the army he began and
went through it as a hawk goes through a flock of
swallows, till he made one heap of their heads
and another heap of their weapons. Then he went
to the castle, caught the king in one hand and the
queen in the other, and putting them under his
two arms brought them out in front of the castle
and killed each with the other.

All was quiet and still at the castle. There
wasn't a man alive to stand up against Gilla na
Grakin, who went to his ship, raised the sails, and
started for Erin. All he heard was the spouting of
whales, the whistling of eels, the calling of gulls,
and the roar of the wind, as the ship rushed back
to the place where he had made it in Erin. When
he reached that place he gave the ship a tip of his
hand, and there before him was the pot of plenty,
and with it the two sticks which he had found on
the shore of the sea when he was going to the
castle of the king of Lochlin.

He left the sticks where he found them, put the
pot on his back, and hurried away to the castle of
Fin MacCumhail.

Fin and all the Fenians of Erin were glad to see
Gilla na Grakin, and Fin thanked him for the work
he had done.

The first part of that night they spent in ease,
the second in sport, the third in a hurried sleep.

Next morning they rose and had breakfast from

the pot. From that day out they hunted for pleasure alone. They had enough and to spare from the pot of plenty.

Another day Conan Maol was outside the castle with Fin, and he said: " Gilla na Grakin will destroy you and me and all of us unless we find some way of putting him to death."

"What do you want him to do now?" asked Fin.

" Let him go," said Conán Maol, to the king of the Flood, "and bring back the cup that is never drained."

Fin went to the castle and called up Gilla na Grakin. " I want you to go now," said he, " to the king of the Flood, and bring me his cup that is never dry."

When he heard Fin's words, Gilla went off without delay; he took a glen at a step, and a hill at a leap, till he came to the sea. There he took up two sticks of wood, threw one across the other, and they became a fine large ship.

Away he sailed in a straight line, listening as he went to the spouting of whales, the whistling of eels and the calling of gulls, and never stopped till he anchored outside the castle of the king of the Flood. There was many a ship at land before him, so he stopped outside them all, and stepped from ship to ship till he reached the shore.

The king of the Flood was giving a great feast that day. Gilla na Grakin went to the castle, but could not enter, so great was the throng. He stood at the door a while, and then called out, " You are an ill-mannered people, not to ask a stranger is he hungry or dry ! "

The king heard these words, and said, " You are right; " and turning to his people said, " Give this stranger the cup till he drinks his fill."

As soon as ever Gilla got the cup in his hands, he made for the ship and never stopped till he put the cup in the hold of the vessel. Then he came on deck, and thought, " It 's no use to take the cup with my swiftness, unless I take it with my ʂtrength."

So back he turned to the castle, and when he reached land, the whole army and all the champions of the king of the Flood stood ready to oppose him. When he came up, he went through them as a hawk through a flock of swallows. He made a heap of their heads in one place, and a heap of their weapons in another, and then went back to the ship without thinking of the king and the queen of the Flood — forgot them.

He raised his sails and went away, listening to music on the sea till he touched land in Erin. Then he took the cup in one hand, struck the ship with the other, turned it into the two sticks which he had found on the shore, and travelled on till he came to the castle of Fin MacCumhail and gave up the cup.

" You 're the best man I have ever had," said Fin; " and I give you my thanks and praise for the work you have done."

In the castle they spent the first part of that night in ease, the second in sport, and the third in a hurried sleep.

Next morning said Fin to the Fenians of Erin, " We need n't leave the house now unless we like. We have the best of eating from the pot, and the best of drinking from the cup. The one is never empty, and the other is never dry, and we 'll go hunting in future only to pass the time for ourselves."

One day Conan Maol was out with Fin a third

time, and said he: " If we don't find some way to
kill Gilla na Grakin, he'll destroy you and me,
and all the Fenians of Erin."

" Well," asked Fin, " where do you want to send
him this time."

" I want him to go to the eastern world, and find
out what was it that left the Gruagach with but the
one hair on his head."

Fin went to the castle, called up Gilla na Grakin,
and said :

" You must go for me now to the eastern world,
to know what was it that left the Gruagach with
the one hair on his head."

" Well," said Gilla, " I never knew that you
wanted to put me to death till this minute; I know
it now. But still so long as I'm in your service I
can't refuse to do your work."

Then Gilla na Grakin stepped out of the castle
door, and away he went to the eastern world. He
took a glen at a step, a hill at a leap, and lochs
and seas at a bound till he entered the Gruagach's
house in the eastern world.

" What is your errand to me," asked the Gruagach, " and why have you come to my house?"

" I have come," said Gilla, " to know what was
it that left you with the one hair on your
head."

" Sit down here and rest yourself to-night, and
if you are a good man, I'll tell you to-morrow,"
said the Gruagach.

When bedtime came the Gruagach said: " There
is an iron harrow there beyond, with teeth on both
sides of it; go now and stretch yourself on that
harrow, and sleep till morning."

When daylight came, the Gruagach was on his
feet, and asked Gilla was he up.

" I am," said he.

After they had eaten breakfast, the Gruagach
went to another room and brought out two iron
loops.   One of these he put on Gilla's neck, and the
other on his own, and then they began to jerk the
loops and pull one another and they fought till
late in the afternoon; neither had the upper hand,
but if one man was weaker than the other, that
man was Gilla na Grakin.

" And now," thought he to himself, " the Gruagach will take my life, and my wife will never know
what became of me."   The thought gave him
strength and power, so up he sprang, and with the
first pull he gave he put the Gruagach to his knees
in the ground, with the second he put him to his
waist, with the third to his shoulders.

" Indeed," said Gilla, " it would be easier for me
to strike the head off you now, than to let you go;
but if I took your head I should n't have my
master's work done."

" If you let me go," said the Gruagach, " I 'll
tell you what happened to me, and why I have but
the one hair on my head."

Gilla set him free, then the two sat down together, and the Gruagach began: —

" I was living here, without trouble or annoy-
ance from any man, till one day a hare ran in,
made an unseemly noise under that table there,
and insulted us.   I was here myself at the time with
my wife and my son and my daughter; and we
had a hound, a beagle, and a black horse.

" The hare ran out from under the table, and I
made after the hare, and my wife and son and
daughter, with the horse and the two dogs, followed
me.

" When the hare was on the top of a hill, I had
almost hold of his hind legs, but I never caught
him.

" When night was near, the hare came to the walls of a great castle, and as he was jumping over, I hit him a blow on the hind leg with a stick, but in he went to the castle.

" Out came an old hag, and screamed, 'Who is it that worried the pet of this castle ! '

" I said it was myself that did it. Then she faced me, and made at me and the fight began between us. We fought all that night, and the next day till near evening. Then she turned around and pulled a Druidic rod out of herself, ran from me and struck my wife and son and daughter and the two hounds and the horse with the Druidic rod and made stones of them.

" Then she turned on me again and there was n't but the one hair left on my head from the desperate fighting, and she looked at me, and said:

" ' I 'll let you go this time but I 'll give you a good payment before you leave.' She caught hold of me then in the grip of her one hand and with the other she took a sharp knife and stripped all the skin and flesh off my back, from my waist to my heels. Then, taking the skin of a rough shaggy goat, she clapped it on to me in place of my own skin and flesh, and told me to go my way.

" I left the old hag and the castle behind, but the skin grew to me and I wear it to this day." And here the Gruagach turned to Gilla na Grakin and showed him the goatskin growing on his body in place of his own skin and flesh.

" Well," said Gilla, when he saw the shaggy back of the Gruagach, " does that hare come here to insult you yet? "

" He does, indeed," said the Gruagach, " but I have n't taken a bite nor a sup off that table since his first visit."

" Let us sit down there now," said Gilla na
Grakin.

They sat down at the table, but they were not
sitting long till the hare came, repeated the insult,
and ran out.

Gilla na Grakin made after the hare, and the
Gruagach after Gilla.

Gilla ran as fast as ever his legs could carry him,
and he was often that near that he used to stretch
his arm out after the hare, and almost catch him;
but he never touched him till near night, when he
was clearing the wall.   Then Gilla caught him by
the two hind legs, and, swinging him over his own
shoulder, dashed him against the wall, tore the
head from the body, and sent it bounding across
the courtyard of the castle.

Out rushed an old hag that minute.   She had
but one tooth and that in her upper jaw, and she
used this tooth for a crutch.

" Who has killed the pet of this castle ! "
shrieked she.

" It was I that killed him," said Gilla na Grakin.
Then the two made at one another, — the hag
and Gilla.   They fought all that night and next
day.   With their fighting they made the hard
rocks soft, and water to spring out through the
middle of them.   All the land of the eastern
world was trembling as the evening drew near,
and if one of the two was getting weak from the
struggle and tired, that one was Gilla na Grakin.
When he saw this he thought to himself, " Is n't it
a pity if an old hag puts me to death, me, who has
put to death many a strong hero."

At this thought he sprang up and seized the
hag.   With the first thrust which he gave her
into the ground he put her to the knees, with

the second to her waist, with the third to her shoulders.

" Now," said the old hag to Gilla, " don't kill me, and I 'll give you the rod of druidism (*enchantment*), which I have between my skin and flesh."

" Oh, you wicked old wretch ! I 'll have that after your death, and no thanks to you," said Gilla. With that he swept the head off of her with a single blow.

Then the head jumped at the body, and tried to get its place again, but Gilla stood between them, and kept the head off till the body was cold. Then he took out the rod of enchantment from between the skin and the flesh, and threw the body and the head of the old hag aside.

The Gruagach came up, and Gilla said, " Show me now the stones which were once your wife and children, your dogs and your horse."

The Gruagach went with him to the stones. Gilla struck each with the rod, and the wife, the son, the daughter, the hounds and the horse of the Gruagach were alive again.

When this was done, Gilla turned to the Gruagach, struck the goatskin from his body, and gave him his own skin and flesh back again with the power of the rod.

When all were restored, they started for the Gruagach's house, and when there the Gruagach said to Gilla na Grakin, —

" Stay here with me till you get your rest. We won't leave this place for a year and a day, and then I 'll go with you to the castle of Fin Mac-Cumhail and give witness to Fin of all that has happened to me and all you have done."

" Oh," said Gilla na Grakin, " I can't stay to rest, I must go now ! "

The Gruagach was so glad that he had got back

all his family and his own flesh that he followed Gilla, and they set out for the castle of Fin Mac-Cumhail in Erin.

They took a glen at a step, a hill at a leap, and the sea at a bound.

Conan Maol, who was outside the castle when they came in sight, ran in and said to Fin, " Gilla na Grakin and the Gruagach are coming, and they 'll destroy all that 's about the castle, and all that 's inside as well ! "

" If they do," said Fin, " it 's your own fault, and you have no one to blame but yourself."

"Well," said Conan Maol, " I 'll lie down here in the cradle, and put a steel cap on my head."

Conan lay down in the cradle. Gilla and the Gruagach came into the castle. The Gruagach sat down near the cradle. Then he said to Fin, " I came here with Gilla na Grakin to bear witness to you of all that has happened to me, and of all he has done."

Then he told Fin the whole story of what they had gone through and what they had done.

With that the Gruagach put his hand behind him and asked : " How old is this child lying here in the cradle ? "

" Only three years," said Fin's wife.

Then the Gruagach took the steel cap between his thumb and fingers, thinking it was the head of the child, and squeezed till the steel cracked with a loud snap, but the child did n't cry.

" Oh, there 's the making of a man in him. If he gets age he 'll be a champion," said the Gruagach.

Next day the Gruagach left Fin's castle and went to his own place and family.

Gilla na Grakin's time was now up, for he had served a year and a day.

Fin went out to wash himself in a spring near

the castle, and when he looked into the spring a spirit spoke up out of the water to him and said:

" You must give back his cup to the king of the Flood, or you must give him battle in its place."

Fin went back to the castle, lamenting the state he was in.

Conan Maol said, " You look like a sorrowful man."

"Why should n't I be?" said Fin. "A spirit spoke to me from the spring outside, and told me I must give back the cup to the king of the Flood, or give him battle in place of it. Now Gilla's time is up, and I don't know what to do."

"Well," said Conan Maol, " do you go now and speak to him, and maybe he 'll do you a good turn."

Fin went to Gilla na Grakin, and told him what happened at the spring.

"My time is up, as you know," said Gilla, " and I cannot serve on time that is past; but if you want me to go, you must watch my wife Scéhide ni Wánanan on Friday night; and in the middle of the night, when she is combing her hair, any request you 'll make of her she can't refuse. The request you 'll make is that she 'll let me go with you to the king of the Flood, to take the cup to his castle and bring it back again."

Fin watched the time closely, and when the middle of Friday night came, he looked through a hole in the door and saw Scéhide combing her hair. Then he asked his request of her.

" Well," answered she, " I can't refuse, but you must promise me to bring back Gilla, dead or alive."

Fin promised her that.

Next morning Fin MacCumhail and Gilla na

Grakin set out for the castle of the king of the Flood, taking the cup with them.

They walked over Erin till they came to the shore of the sea. There Gilla caught up two pieces of wood, and putting one across the other, struck them a tip of his fingers, and out of them rose a fine ship. He and Fin went on board, sailed away, and never stopped till they cast anchor outside all the ships, under the castle of the king of the Flood. The two walked on from deck to deck till they stood on shore.

They went a short distance from the castle of the king and pitched a tent.

Said Gilla to Fin, "Now we are hungry, and I must find food for you and myself."

So Gilla na Grakin went to the castle and asked food of the king of the Flood.

"You 'll get nothing to eat from me. I have no food in this place to give you or the like of you; but there is a wild bull in the wood outside. Find him: if you kill him, you 'll have something to eat; if not you 'll go fasting," said the king of the Flood to Gilla na Grakin.

Gilla went out to the wood, and when the wild bull saw a man coming towards him he drove his horns into the ground, and put an acre of land over his own back. Then he threw up an oak-tree, roots and all, till it nearly reached the sky, and made at Gilla na Grakin. But if he did, Gilla was ready for him and faced him, and when the bull came up, he caught him by the horns and threw him to the ground; then putting a foot on one horn, he took the other in his two hands, split the bull from muzzle to tail, and made two halves of him.

Gilla carried the carcass to the tent, and when

he had taken off the skin he said to Fin, "We have no pot to boil the meat in.   Well, I'll go to the king again."

So off he went and knocked at the castle door.

" What do you want now? " asked the king.

" I want a pot," said Gilla, " to boil the wild bull."

" Well," said the king, " I have no pot for you but that big pot back in the yard, in which we boil stuff for the pigs.   I'll give you the loan of that if you are able to carry it."

" It's good to get that itself from a bad person," said Gilla na Grakin, and away he went to look for the pot behind the castle.

At last he found it, and when he put it down at the tent he said to Fin, " We have nothing now to boil the pot with, nothing to make a fire."

Then he went a third time to the castle, knocked at the door, and out came the king.   " What do you want now? " asked he.

" Fire to boil the bull."

" Go to the wood and get firewood for yourself, or do without it.   You'll get no firewood from me," said the king of the Flood.

Gilla went out, got plenty of wood and boiled the whole bull.

"We are well off now," said he to Fin; " we have plenty to eat."

Next morning Gilla na Grakin went to the castle and knocked.

"Who is that? " asked the king, without opening the door.

" I want no chat nor questions from you," said Gilla, " but get me a breakfast."

" I have no breakfast now," said the king; " but wait a minute and you 'll get a hot breakfast from me."

That moment the signal was sounded for the armies of the king of the Flood to take Gilla na Grakin and his master.

When the armies stood ready Gilla began and went through them as a hawk through sparrows. He made one heap of their heads and another of their weapons, — did n't leave a man living.   Then he went into the castle and taking the king of the Flood in one hand and the queen in the other, he killed each of them against the other.

Now all was quiet at the castle.   Gilla na Grakin struck the tent and went to the ship with Fin MacCumhail, who had the cup that was never dry.

They raised the sails and went over the sea toward Erin, till they saw a large ship on one side of them.

" If it 's going to help us that ship is," said Fin, " 't is all the better for us, but if 't is going against us she is, that 's the bad part of it."

As the ship came near, Gilla na Grakin looked at her sharply, and said to Fin, " I think it 's Lun Dubh that 's on that ship."

" Well," said Fin, " may be he 'll not know you in a strange dress."

When Lun Dubh came alongside, he called out: " I know you well, and it 's not by your dress that I know you, Césa MacRi na Tulach."   Then Lun Dubh sprang on deck, raised his hand, struck Gilla, and stretched him dead.

Fin sailed away with the body of Gilla na Grakin, and when he came in sight of the shore of Erin he raised a black flag; for he had promised Gilla's wife to raise a white flag if her husband was well, but a black one if he was dead.

When he came to the shore, Scéhide ni Wánanan was there before him, and she had a large, roomy box. When she saw Fin she said, "You have him dead with you?"

"I have," said Fin.

"What will you do with him now?" asked she.

"I will bury him decently," said Fin.

"You will not," said she; "you will put him in this box."

Then Fin put him in the box. She went aside and got some fresh shamrock and went into the box with Gilla. Then she told Fin to push the box out to sea, and putting down the cover fastened it inside.

Fin pushed the box out into the sea, and away it went driven by wind and waves, till one day Scéhide looked out through a hole and saw two sparrows flying and a dead one between them. The two living sparrows let the dead one down on an island. Soon they rose up again, and the dead one was living.

Said Scéhide to herself, "There might be something on that island that would cure my husband as it cured the dead bird."

Now the sea put the box in on the island. Scéhide unfastened the cover, came out, and walked around the island. Nothing could she find but a small spring of water in a rock. "It's in this the cure may be," thought she, as she looked at the water. Then taking off one of her shoes she put it full of the water, took it to the box, and poured it on Gilla na Grakin. That moment he stood up alive and well.

Gilla walked along the shore till he found two pieces of wood. He threw one across the other, gave them a tip of his hand, a fine large ship stood there at the shore, and in it he sailed with Scéhide back to Erin.

When they landed he turned the vessel into two sticks again with a tip of the hand, and set out with his wife for the castle of Fin MacCumhail in TirConal.

They came to the castle of Fin at midnight. Gilla knocked and said, "Put my wages out to me."

"Well," said Fin inside, "there is no man, alive or dead, that has wages on me but Gilla na Grakin, and I would rather see that fellow here than the wages of three men."

"Well, rise up now and you 'll see him," said Gilla.

Fin rose up, saw his man, gave him his wages with thanks and Gilla departed.

At the break of day they saw a great house before them. A man walked out with a kerchief bound on his head.

When Gilla na Grakin came up, he knew the man, and raising his hand, struck him dead with a blow.

"I have satisfaction on Lun Dubh, now," said Gilla to the wife. The two went into the house and stayed there, and may be there yet for anything we know. We are the luck and they are the winners.

FIN MACCUMHAIL.

THE SEVEN BROTHERS AND THE KING OF FRANCE.

WHEN Fin MacCumhail with seven companies of the Fenians of Erin was living at Tara of the Kings, he went hunting one day with the seven companies; and while out on the mountains seven young men came towards him and when they came up and stood before him he asked their names of them.

Each gave his name in turn, beginning with the eldest, and their names were Strong, son of Strength; Wise, son of Wisdom; Builder, son of Builder; Whistler, son of Whistler; Guide, son of Guide; Climber, son of Climber; Thief, son of Thief.

The seven young men pleased Fin; they were looking for service, so he hired them for a year and a day.

When Fin and the Fenians of Erin went home that night from the hunt there was a message at the castle before them from the king of France to Fin MacCumhail and the Fenians of Erin, asking them to come over to him on a most important affair.

Fin held a council straightway and said, " France is a thousand miles from this and the sea between it and Erin; how can we go to the king of France? "

Then Strong, son of Strength, spoke up and said: " What is the use of hiring us if we can't do this work and the like of it? If you'll make a ship here, or in any place, I'll pull it in the sea."

"And I," said Builder, "will make a ship fit for you or any king on earth with one blow of this axe in my hand."

"That's what I want," said Fin, "and now do you make that ship for me."

"I will," said Builder.

"Well," said Strong, "I'll put your ship in the sea."

Builder made the ship there at Tara of the Kings and then Strong brought it to the seashore and put it in the water. Fin and the Fenians of Erin went on board, and Guide took the ship from Erin to France.

When Fin and his men went to the king of France he was glad to see them and said:

"I'll tell you the reason now I asked you here, and the business I have with you. This time three years ago my wife had a son, two years ago a second, one year ago a third, and the neighbors' wives are thinking she'll have another child soon. Immediately they were born the three were taken away, and I want you to save the fourth; for we all think it will be taken from us like the other three. When each one of the others was sleeping, a hand came down the chimney to the cradle and took the child away with it up the chimney. There is meat and drink in plenty in that room for you and the Fenians of Erin. My only request is that you'll watch the child."

"We'll do that," said Fin, and he went into the chamber with men enough to watch and the seven brothers with him. Then the seven said: "Do you and the men go to sleep for yourselves, and we'll do the watching."

So Fin and the men went to sleep. The child was born early in the evening and put in the cradle. At the dead of night Wise said to Strong: "Now is your time; the hand is near; keep your eye on it."

Soon he saw the hand coming lower and lower and moving towards the child; and when it was going into the cradle, Strong caught the hand and it drew him up nearly to the top of the chimney. Then he pulled it down to the ashes; again it drew him up.

They were that way all night, — the hand drawing Strong almost to the top of the chimney and out of the house and Strong dragging the hand down to the hearth. They were up and down the chimney till break of day; and every stone in the castle of the king of France was trembling in its place from the struggle.

But at break of day Strong tore from its shoulder the arm with the hand, and there was peace. Now all rose up at the castle. The king came and was glad when he saw the child.

Then Fin spoke up and said: "We have done no good thing yet till we bring back the other three to you."

Wise spoke up and said: "I know very well where the other three are, and I'll show you the place."

So all set out and they followed him to the castle of Mal MacMulcan and there they saw the three sons of the King of France carrying water to MacMulcan to cool the shoulder from which the arm had been torn by Strong.

Then Wise said to Climber: "Now is your time to take the children away; for we can do it without being seen; but if Mal MacMulcan were to see the children going from him, he'd destroy the whole world. But as it is when he finds the children are gone, he has a sister there near himself, and he'll break her head against the wall of the castle."

Then Climber took a clew from his pocket and threw it over the walls of the castle, and the walls were so high that no bird of the air could fly over them. Then they fixed a rope ladder on the castle. Wise, Guide, and Climber went up the ladder and at break of day they brought away the three children and gave them to the king of France that morning. And the king of France was so glad when he saw his three sons that he said to Fin: "I will give you your ship full of the most precious stuffs in my kingdom."

" I will take nothing for myself," said Fin; "but do you give what you like to my seven young men who have done the work; " and the seven said they wouldn't take anything while they were serving with him. So Fin took the present from the king of France and set sail for Erin with the Fenians and the seven young men.

While they were on the way to Erin they saw the sea raging after them. Wise, son of Wisdom, said: "That is Mal MacMulcan coming to get satisfaction out of us."

Then MacMulcan caught hold of the ship by the stern and pulled it down till the masts touched the sea. Strong caught him by the left remaining hand, and the two began to fight, and at last Strong pulled him on to the deck of the ship.

"Our ship will be sunk," said Wise, " and Fin with the Fenians of Erin and the seven of us will be drowned unless you make a flail out of Mac-

Mulcan and thrash the head off his body on the deck of the ship."

Strong made a flail out of MacMulcan and killed him, and the sea was filled with blood in a minute of time. Then the ship moved on without harm till they came to the same spot in Erin from which they had sailed.

When Fin came to the place where he had hired the seven young men the year and a day were over. He paid them their hire and they left him. Then he came to his own castle at Tara of the Kings.

One day Fin went out walking alone, and he met an old hag by the way. She spoke up to him and asked: "Would you play a game of cards with me?"

"I would," said Fin, "if I had the means of playing."

The old hag pulled out a pack of cards and said: "Here you have the means of playing as many games as you like."

They sat down and played; Fin got the first game on the old woman. Then she said, "Put the sentence on me now."

"I will not," said Fin; "I'll do nothing till we play another game."

They played again and she won the second game. Then she said to Fin, "You will have to go and bring here for me the head of Curucha na Gras and the sword that guards his castle; and I won't give you leave to take away any of your men with you but one, and he is the worst of them all,—'Iron back without action,' and the time for your journey is a year and a day. Now what is your sentence on me?" said the old hag.

"You'll put one foot," said Fin, "on the top of my castle in Tara of the Kings, and the other on

a hill in Mayo, and you 'll stand with your back to
the wind and your face to the storm, a sheaf of
wheat on the ground before the gate will be all
you 'll have to eat, and any grain that will be
blown out of it, if you catch that you 'll have it,
and you 'll be that way till I come back."

So Fin went away with himself and " Iron back
without action." And when they had gone as far
as a large wood that was by the roadside, a thick
fog came on them, and rain, and they sat down at
the edge of the wood and waited. Soon they saw
a red-haired boy with a bow and arrows shooting
birds, and whenever he hit a bird he used to put
the arrow through its two eyes and not put a drop
of blood on its feathers.

And when the red boy came near Fin, he drew
his bow, sent an arrow through " Iron back without
action," and put the life out of him.

When he did that Fin said, " You have left me
without any man, though this was the worst of all
I have."

" You 'd better hire me," said the red boy;
" you 've lost nothing, for you were without a man
when you had that fellow the same as you are now."

So Fin hired the red boy and asked him his
name. " I won't tell you that," said he, " but do
you put the name on me that 'll please yourself."

" Well," said Fin, " since I met you in the rain
and the mist I 'll call you Misty."

" That 'll be my name while I 'm with you," said
the red boy, " and now we 'll cast lots to see which
of us will carry the other; " and the lot fell upon
Misty. He raised Fin on his back to carry him,
and the first leap he took was six miles, and every
step a mile, and he went on without stopping till
he was in the Western World. When they came

to the castle of Curucha na Gras, Fin and Misty put up a tent for themselves and they were hungry enough after the long road, and Misty said, " I will go and ask Curucha for something to eat." He went to the castle and put a fighting blow on the door. Curucha came out and Misty asked him for bread.

" I would n't give you the leavings of my pigs," said Curucha.

Misty turned and left him, but on the way he met the bakers bringing bread from the bake house and he caught all their loaves from them and ran home to Fin. " We have plenty to eat now," said Misty, " but nothing at all to drink. I must go to Curucha to know will he give us something to drink."

He went a second time to the castle, put a fighting blow on the door, and out came Curucha.

" What do you want this time? " asked he.

" I want drink for myself and my master, Fin MacCumhail."

" You 'll get no drink from me. I would n't give you the dirty ditch-water that 's outside my castle."

Misty turned to go home, but on the way he met twelve boys each carrying the full of his arms of bottles of wine. He took every bottle from them, and it was n't long till he was in the tent.

" Now we can eat and drink our fill."

" We can indeed," said Fin. Next morning Misty put another fighting blow on the door of the castle. Out flew Curucha with his guardian sword in his hand, and he made at Misty. With the first blow he gave him, he took an ear off his head.

Misty sprang back, drew his bow, and sent an

arrow into Curucha's breast. It flew out through his head and he fell lifeless on the ground. Then Misty drew his knife, cut off the head, and carried the head and the sword to Fin MacCumhail, and Fin was glad to get them both.

"Take the head," said Misty, " and put it on top of the holly bush that's out here above us." Fin put the head on the holly bush, and the minute he put it there the head burnt the bush to the earth, and the earth to the clay.

Then they took the best horse that could be found about Curucha's castle, Fin sat on the horse, with the sword and head in front of him; and Misty followed behind.

They went their way and never stopped till they came to the place where Misty sent the arrow through "Iron back without action" and killed him. When they came to that spot, Misty asked Fin would he tell him a story, and Fin answered, " I have no story to tell except that we are in the place now where you killed my man."

"Oh, then," said Misty, " I'm glad you put that in my mind for I'll give him back to you now." So they went and took " Iron back without action " out of the ground; then Misty struck him with a rod of enchantment which he had, and brought life into him again.

Then Misty turned to Fin and said: " I am a brother of the seven boys who went with you to save the children of the king of France. I was too young for action at that time, but my mother sent me here now as a gift to help you and tell you what to do. When you go to the hag she'll ask you for the sword, but you'll not give it, you'll only show it to her. And when she has seen the sword she'll ask for the head. And you'll not give the head to her either, you'll only show it; and when she sees the head, she'll open her mouth with joy at seeing the head of her brother; and when you see her open her mouth be sure to strike her on the breast with the head; and if you don't do that, the whole world wouldn't be able to kill her."

Then Fin left Misty where he met him and with "Iron back without action" he made for Tara of the Kings.

When he came in front of the old hag she asked him had he the gifts. Fin said he had. She asked for the sword but she didn't get it, Fin only showed it to her. Then she asked for the head, and when she saw the head, she opened her mouth with delight at seeing the head of her brother.

While she stood there with open mouth gazing, Fin picked out the mark and struck her on the breast with the head. She fell to the ground; they left her there dead and went into the castle.

BLACK, BROWN, AND GRAY.

ON a day Fin MacCumhail was near Tara of the Kings, south of Ballyshannon, hunting with seven companies of the Fenians of Erin.

During the day they saw three strange men coming towards them, and Fin said to the Fenians: "Let none of you speak to them, and if they have good manners they'll not speak to you nor to any man till they come to me."

When the three men came up, they said nothing till they stood before Fin himself. Then he asked what their names were and what they wanted. They answered: —

"Our names are Dubh, Dun, and Glasán [Black, Brown, and Gray]. We have come to find Fin MacCumhail, chief of the Fenians of Erin, and take service with him."

Fin was so well pleased with their looks that he brought them home with him that evening and called them his sons. Then he said, "Every man who comes to this castle must watch the first night for me, and since three of you have come together, each will watch one third of the night. You'll cast lots to see who'll watch first and second."

Fin had the trunk of a tree brought, three equal parts made of it, and one given to each of the men.

Then he said, "When each of you begins his watch he will set fire to his own piece of wood, and so long as the wood burns he will watch."

The lot fell to Dubh to go on the first watch.

Dubh set fire to his log, then went out around the castle, the dog Bran with him. He wandered on, going further and further from the castle, and Bran after him. At last he saw a bright light and went towards it. When he came to the place where the light was burning, he saw a large house. He entered the house and when inside saw a great company of most strange looking men, drinking out of a single cup.

The chief of the party, who was sitting on a high place, gave the cup to the man nearest him; and when he had drunk his fill out of it, he passed it to his neighbor, and so on to the last.

While the cup was going the round of the company, the chief said, " This is the great cup that was taken from Fin MacCumhail a hundred years ago; and as much as each man wishes to drink he always gets from it, and no matter how many men there may be, or what they wish for, they always have their fill."

Dubh sat near the door on the edge of the crowd, and when the cup came to him he drank a little, then slipped out and hurried away in the dark; when he came to the fountain at the castle of Fin MacCumhail, his log was burned.

As the second lot had fallen on Dun, it was now his turn to watch, so he set fire to his log and went out, in the place of Dubh, with the dog Bran after him.

Dun walked on through the night till he saw a fire. He went towards it, and when he had come near he saw a large house, which he entered; and when inside he saw a crowd of strange looking men, fighting. They were ferocious, wonderful to look at, and fighting wildly.

The chief, who had climbed on the crossbeams of the house to escape the uproar and struggle, called out to the crowd below: "Stop fighting now; for I have a better gift than the one you have lost this night." And putting his hand behind his belt, he drew out a knife and held it before them, saying: "Here is the wonderful knife, the small knife of division, that was stolen from Fin MacCumhail a hundred years ago, and if you cut on a bone with the knife, you'll get the finest meat in the world, and as much of it as ever your hearts can wish for."

Then he passed down the knife and a bare bone to the man next him, and the man began to cut; and off came slices of the sweetest and best meat in the world.

The knife and the bone passed from man to man till they came to Dun, who cut a slice off the bone, slipped out unseen, and made for Fin's castle as fast as his two legs could carry him through the darkness and over the ground.

When he was by the fountain at the castle, his part of the log was burned and his watch at an end.

Now Glasán set fire to his stick of wood and went out on his watch and walked forward till he saw the light and came to the same house that Dubh and Dun had visited. Looking in he saw the place full of dead bodies, and thought, "There must be some great wonder here. If I lie down in the midst of these and put some of them over me to hide myself, I shall be able to see what is going on."

He lay down and pulled some of the bodies over himself. He wasn't there long when he saw an old hag coming into the house. She had but one leg, one arm, and one upper tooth, which was as long as her leg and served her in place of a crutch.

When inside the door she took up the first corpse she met and threw it aside; it was lean. As she went on she took two bites out of every fat corpse she met, and threw every lean one aside.

She had her fill of flesh and blood before she came to Glasán; and as soon as she had that, she dropped down on the floor, lay on her back, and went to sleep.

Every breath she drew, Glasán was afraid she'd drag the roof down on top of his head, and every time she let a breath out of her he thought she'd sweep the roof off the house.

Then he rose up, looked at her, and wondered at the bulk of her body. At last he drew his sword, hit her a slash, and if he did, three young giants sprang forth.

Glasán killed the first giant, the dog Bran killed the second, and the third ran away.

Glasán now hurried back, and when he reached the fountain at Fin's castle, his log of wood was burned, and day was dawning.

When all had risen in the morning, and the Fenians of Erin came out, Fin said to Dubh, " Have you anything new or wonderful to tell me after the night's watching?"

" I have," said Dubh; " for I brought back the drinking-cup that you lost a hundred years ago. I was out in the darkness watching. I walked on, and the dog Bran with me till I saw a light. When I came to the light I found a house, and in the house a company feasting. The chief was a very old man, and sat on a high place above the rest. He took out the cup and said: ' This is the cup that was stolen from Fin MacCumháil a hundred years ago, and it is always full of the best drink in the world; and when one of you has drunk from the cup pass it on to the next.'

" They drank and passed the cup till it came to me.   I took it and hurried back.   When I came here, my log was burned and my watch was finished.   Here now is the cup for you," said Dubh to Fin MacCumhail.

Fin praised him greatly for what he had done, and turning to Dun said: "Now tell us what happened in your watch."

" When my turn came I set fire to the log which you gave me, and walked on; the dog Bran following, till I saw a light.   When I came to the light, I found a house in which was a crowd of people, all fighting except one very old man on a high place above the rest.   He called to them for peace, and told them to be quiet.   ' For,' said he, ' I have a better gift for you than the one you lost this night,' and he took out the small knife of division with a bare bone, and said: ' This is the knife that was stolen from Fin MacCumhail, a hundred years ago, and whenever you cut on the bone with the knife, you 'll get your fill of the best meat on earth.'

" Then he handed the knife and the bone to the man nearest him, who cut from it all the meat he wanted, and then passed it to his neighbor.   The knife went from hand to hand till it came to me, then I took it, slipped out, and hurried away. When I came to the fountain, my log was burned, and here are the knife and bone for you."

" You have done a great work, and deserve my best praise," said Fin.   " We are sure of the best eating and drinking as long as we keep the cup and the knife."

" Now what have you seen in your part of the night?" said Fin to Glasán.

" I went out," said Glasán, "with the dog Bran,

and walked on till I saw a light, and when I came
to the light I saw a house, which I entered. Inside
were heaps of dead men, killed in fighting, and I
wondered greatly when I saw them. At last I lay
down in the midst of the corpses, put some of
them over me and waited to see what would
happen.

"Soon an old hag came in at the door, she had
but one arm, one leg, and the one tooth out of
her upper jaw, and that tooth as long as her leg,
and she used it for a crutch as she hobbled along.
She threw aside the first corpse she met and took
two bites out of the second, — for she threw every
lean corpse away and took two bites out of every
fat one. When she had eaten her fill, she lay down
on her back in the middle of the floor and went
to sleep. I rose up then to look at her, and every
time she drew a breath I was in dread she would
bring down the roof of the house on the top of my
head, and every time she let a breath out of her,
I thought she'd sweep the roof from the building,
so strong was the breath of the old hag.

"Then I drew my sword and cut her with a
blow, but if I did three young giants sprang up
before me. I killed the first, Bran killed the second, but the third escaped. I walked away then,
and when I was at the fountain outside, daylight
had come and my log was burned."

"Between you and me," said Fin, "it would
have been as well if you had let the old hag alone.
I am greatly in dread the third young giant will
bring trouble on us all."

For twenty-one years Fin MacCumhail and the
Fenians of Erin hunted for sport alone. They had
the best of eating from the small knife of division,
and the best of drinking from the cup that was
never dry.

At the end of twenty-one years Dubh, Dun, and Glasán went away, and one day, as Fin and the Fenians of Erin were hunting on the hills and mountains, they saw a Fear Ruadh (a red haired man) coming toward them.

"There is a bright looking man coming this way," said Fin, "and don't you speak to him."

"Oh, what do we care for him?" asked Conan Maol.

"Don't be rude to a stranger," said Fin.

The Fear Ruadh came forward and spoke to no man till he stood before Fin.

"What have you come for?" asked Fin.

"To find a master for twenty-one years."

"What wages do you ask?" inquired Fin.

"No wages but this, — that if I die before the twenty-one years have passed, I shall be buried on Inis Caol (Light Island)."

"I'll give you those wages," said Fin, and he hired the Fear Ruadh for twenty-one years.

He served Fin for twenty years to his satisfaction; but toward the end of the twenty-first year he fell into a decline, became an old man, and died.

When the Fear Ruadh was dead, the Fenians of Erin said that not a step would they go to bury him; but Fin declared that he wouldn't break his word for any man, and must take the corpse to Inis Caol.

Fin had an old white horse which he had turned out to find a living for himself as he could on the hillsides and in the woods. And now he looked for the horse and found that he had become younger than older in looks since he had put him out. So he took the old white horse and tied a coffin, with the body of the Fear Ruadh in it, on his back. Then they started him on ahead

and away he went followed by Fin and twelve men
of the Fenians of Erin.

When they came to the temple on Inis Caol
there were no signs of the white horse and the
coffin; but the temple was open and in went Fin
and the twelve.

There were seats for each man inside. They
sat down and rested awhile and then Fin tried to
to rise but could n't. He told the men to rise, but
the twelve were fastened to the seats, and the seats
to the ground, so that not a man of them could
come to his feet.

" Oh, " said Fin, " I 'm in dread there is some
evil trick played on us."

At that moment the Fear Ruadh stood before
them in all his former strength and youth and said:
" Now is the time for me to take satisfaction
out of you for my mother and brothers," Then
one of the men said to Fin, " Chew your thumb
to know is there any way out of this."

Fin chewed his thumb to know what should he
do. When he knew, he blew the great whistle with
his two hands; which was heard by Donogh Kam-
cosa and Diarmuid O'Duivne.

The Fear Ruadh fell to and killed three of the
men; but before he could touch the fourth
Donogh and Diarmuid were there, and put an end
to him. Now all were free, and Fin with the nine
men went back to their castle south of Ballyshannon.

FIN MACCUMHAIL AND THE SON OF THE KING OF ALBA.

ON a day Fin went out hunting with his dog Bran, on Knock an Ar; and he killed so much game that he did n't know what to do with it or how to bring it home. As he stood looking and thinking, all at once he saw a man running towards him, with a rope around his waist so long that half his body was covered with it; and the man was of such size that, as he ran, Fin could see the whole world between his legs and nothing between his head and the sky. When he came up, the man saluted Fin, who answered him most kindly. "Where are you going?" asked Fin. "I am out looking for a master." "Well," said Fin, "I am in sore need of a man; what can you do?" "Do you see this rope on my body? Whatever this rope will bind I can carry." "If that is true," said Fin, "you are the man I want. Do you see the game on this hillside?" "I do," said the man. "Well, put that into the rope and carry it to my castle."

The man put all the game into the rope, made a great bundle, and threw it on his back.

"Show me the way to the castle now," said he. Fin started on ahead, and though he ran with all his might, he could not gain one step on the man who followed with the game. The sentry on guard at the castle saw the man running while yet far off. He stepped inside the gate and said: "There is a man coming with a load on his back as big as a mountain." Before he could come out again to his place the man was there and the load off his back. When the game came to the ground, it shook the castle to its foundations. Next day the man was sent to herd cows for a time, and while he was gone, Conán Maol said to Fin: " If you don't put this cowherd to death, he will destroy all the Fenians of Erin." " How could I put such a good man to death?" asked Fin. " Send him," said Conán, " to sow corn on the brink of a lake in the north of Erin. Now, in that lake lives a serpent that never lets a person pass, but swallows every man that goes that way." Fin agreed to this, and the next morning after breakfast he called the man, gave him seven bullocks, a plough, and a sack of grain, and sent him to the lake in the north of Erin to sow corn. When he came to the lake, the man started to plough, drew one furrow. The lake began to boil up, and as he was coming back, making the second furrow, the serpent was on the field before him and swallowed the seven bullocks and the plough up to the handles. But the man held fast to what he had in his two hands, gave a pull, and dragged the plough and six of the bullocks out of the belly of the serpent. The seventh one remained inside. The serpent went at him and they fought for seven days and nights. At the end of that time the serpent was as tame as a cat, and the man drove him and the six bullocks home before him.

When he was in sight of Fin's castle, the sentry at the gate ran in and cried: " That cowherd is coming with the size of a mountain before him! " " Run out," said Conán Maol, " and tell him to tie the serpent to that oak out there."

They ran out, and the man tied the serpent to the oak-tree, then came in and had a good supper.

Next morning the man went out to herd cows

as before. "Well," said Conán Maol to Fin, "if you don't put this man to death, he'll destroy you and me and all the Fenians of Erin."

"How could I put such a man to death?"

"There is," said Conán, "a bullock in the north of Erin, and he drives fog out of himself for seven days and then he draws it in for seven other days. To-morrow is the last day for drawing it in. If any one man comes near, he'll swallow him alive."

When the cowherd came to supper in the evening, Fin said to him: "I am going to have a feast and need fresh beef. Now there is a bullock in that same valley by the lake in the north of Erin where you punished the serpent; and if you go there and bring the bullock to me, you'll have my thanks."

"I'll go," said the man, "the first thing after breakfast in the morning."

So off he went next morning; and when he came near the valley, he found the bullock asleep and drawing in the last of the fog; and soon he found himself going in with it. So he caught hold of a great oak-tree for safety. The bullock woke up then and saw him, and letting a roar out of himself, faced him, and gave him a pitch with his horn which sent him seven miles over the top of a wood. And when he fell to the ground, the bullock was on him again before he had time to rise, and gave him another pitch which sent him back and broke three ribs in his body.

"This will never do," said the man, as he rose, and pulling up an oak-tree by the roots for a club, he faced the bullock. And there they were at one another for five days and nights, till the bullock was as tame as a cat and the man drove him home to Fin's castle.

The sentry saw them coming and ran inside the gate with word. " Tell the man to tie the bullock to that oak-tree beyond," said Conán. "We don't want him near this place." The cowherd tied the bullock, and told Fin to send four of the best butchers in Erin to kill him with an axe; and the four of them struck him one after another and any of them could n't knock him.

"Give me an axe," said the man to the butchers. They gave him the axe, and the first stroke he gave, he knocked the bullock. Then they began to skin him; but the man did n't like the way they were doing the work, so he took his sword and had three quarters of the bullock skinned before they could skin one.

Next morning the cowherd went out with the cows; but he was n't long gone when Conán Maol came to Fin and said: " If you don't put an end to that man, he 'll soon put an end to you and to me and to all of us, so there won't be a man of the Fenians of Erin left alive."

" How could I put an end to a man like him? " asked Fin.

"There is in the north of Erin," said Conán, " a wild sow who has two great pigs of her own; and she and her two pigs have bags of poison in their tails; and when they see any man, they run at him and shake their poison bags; and if the smallest drop of the poison touches him, it is death to him that minute. And, if by any chance he should escape the wild sow and the pigs, there is a fox-man called the Gruagach, who has but one eye and that in the middle of his forehead. The Gruagach carries a club of a ton weight, and if the cowherd gets one welt of that club, he 'll never trouble the Fenians of Erin again."

Next morning Fin called up the cowherd and

said, "I am going to have a feast in this castle, and
I would like to have some fresh pork.   There is a
wild sow in the north of Erin with two pigs, and if
you bring her to me before the feast, you 'll have
my thanks."

"I 'll go and bring her to you," said the cowherd.
So after breakfast he took his sword, went to the
north of Erin, and stole up to the sow and two
pigs, and whipped the tails off the three of them,
before they knew he was in it.   Then he faced the
wild sow and fought with her for four days and
five nights, and on the morning of the fifth day he
knocked her dead.   At the last blow, his sword
stuck in her backbone and he could n't draw it
out.   But with one pull he broke the blade, and
stood there over her with only the hilt in his hand.
Then he put his foot on one of her jaws, took the
other in his hands, and splitting her evenly from
the nose to the tail, made two halves of her.

He threw one half on his shoulder; and that
minute the big Gruagach with one eye in his head
came along and made an offer of his club at him
to kill him.   But the cowherd jumped aside, and
catching the Gruagach by one of his legs, threw
him up on to the half of the wild sow on his shoulder,
and taking the other half of her from the ground,
clapped that on the top of the Gruagach, and ran
away to Fin's castle as fast as his legs could carry
him.

The sentry at the castle gate ran in and said:
" The cowherd is running to the castle, and the size
of a mountain on his back."   " Go out now," said
Conán Maol, " and stop him where he is, or he 'll
throw down the castle if he comes here with the
load that 's on him."   But before the sentry was
back at his place, the cowherd was at the gate
shaking the load off his back and the castle to its

foundations, so that every dish and vessel in it was broken to bits.

The Gruagach jumped from the ground, rubbed his legs and every part of him that was sore from the treatment he got. He was so much in dread of the cowherd that he ran with all the strength that was in him, and never stopped to look back till he was in the north of Erin.

Next morning the cowherd went out with the cows, drove them back in the evening, and while picking the thigh-bone of a bullock for his supper, Oscar, son of Oisin, the strongest man of the Fenians of Erin, came up to him and took hold of the bone to pull it from his hand. The cowherd held one end and Oscar the other, and pulled till they made two halves of the bone. "What did you carry away?" asked the cowherd. "What I have in my hand," said Oscar. "And I kept what I held in my fist," said the cowherd. "There is that for you now," said Oscar, and he hit him a slap.

The cowherd said no word in answer, but next morning he asked his wages of Fin. "Oh, then," said Fin, "I'll pay you and welcome, for you are the best man I have ever had or met with."

Then the cowherd went away to Cahirciveen in Kerry where he had an enchanted castle. But before he went he invited Fin MacCumhail and the Fenians of Erin to have a great feast with him. "For," said he to Fin, "I'm not a cowherd at all, but the son of the king of Alba, and I'll give you good cheer."

When the Fenians came to the place, they found the finest castle that could be seen. There were three fires in each room and seven spits at every fire. When they had gone and sat down in their places, there was but one fire in each room.

" Rise up, every man of you," said Fin, " or we are lost; for this is an enchanted place."

They tried to rise, but each man was fastened to his seat, and the seat to the floor; and not one of them could stir. Then the last fire went out and they were in darkness.

"Chew your thumb," said Conán to Fin, "and try is there any way out of here." Fin chewed his thumb and knew what trouble they were in. Then he put his two hands into his mouth and blew the old-time whistle. And this whistle was heard by Pogán and Ceolán, two sons of Fin who were in the North at that time, one fishing and the other hurling.

When they heard the whistle, they said: " Our father and the Fenians of Erin are in trouble." And they faced towards the sound and never stopped till they knocked at the door of the enchanted castle of the son of Alba at Cahirciveen.

" Who is there? " asked Fin.

" Your two sons," said one of them.

" Well," said Fin, " we are in danger of death to-night. That cowherd I had in my service was no cowherd at all, but the son of the king of Alba; and his father has said that he will not eat three meals off one table without having my head. There is an army now on the road to kill us to-night. There is no way in or out of this castle but by one ford, and to that ford the army of the king of Alba is coming."

The two sons of Fin went out at nightfall and stood in the ford before the army. The son of the king of Alba knew them well, and calling each by name, said: "Won't you let us pass? " " We will not," said they; and then the fight began. The two sons of Fin MacCumhail, Pogán and Ceolán, destroyed the whole army and killed every man except the son of the king of Alba.

After the battle the two went back to their
father. "We have destroyed the whole army at
the ford," said they.

"There is a greater danger ahead," said Fin.
"There is an old hag coming with a little pot. She
will dip her finger in the pot, touch the lips of
the dead men, and bring the whole army to life.
But first of all there will be music at the ford, and
if you hear the music, you 'll fall asleep. Now go,
but if you do not overpower the old hag, we are
lost."

"We 'll do the best we can," said the two sons
of Fin.

They were not long at the ford when one said,
"I am falling asleep from that music." "So am
I," said the other. "Knock your foot down on
mine," said the first. The other kicked his foot
and struck him, but no use. Then each took his
spear and drove it through the foot of the other,
but both fell asleep in spite of the spears.

The old hag went on touching the lips of the
dead men, who stood up alive; and she was cross-
ing the ford at the head of the army when she
stumbled over the two sleeping brothers and spilt
what was in the pot over their bodies.

They sprang up fresh and well, and picking up
two stones of a ton weight each that were there in
the ford, they made for the champions of Alban and
never stopped till they killed the last man of them;
and then they killed the old hag herself.

Pogán and Ceolán then knocked at the door of
e castle.

"Who 's there?" asked Fin.

"Your two sons," said they; "and we have killed
champions of Alban and the old hag as

" You have more to do yet," said Fin.   " There
are three kings in the north of Erin who have
three silver goblets.   These kings are holding a
feast in a fort to-day.   You must go and cut the
heads off the three, put their blood in the goblets
and bring them here.   When you come, rub the
blood on the keyhole of the door and it will open
before you.   When you come in, rub the seats
and we shall all be free."

The three goblets of blood were brought to
Cahirciveen, the door of the castle flew open, and
light came into every room.   The brothers rubbed
blood on the chairs of all the Fenians of Erin and
freed them all, except Conán Maol, who had no
chair, but sat on the floor with his back to the wall.
When they came to him the last drop of blood was
gone.

All the Fenians of Erin were hurrying past,
anxious to escape, and paid no heed to Conán,
who had never a good word in his mouth for any
man.   Then Conán turned to Diarmuid, and said:
" If a woman were here in place of me, you
would n't leave her to die this way."   Then Diarmuid turned, took him by one hand, and Goll
MacMorna by the other, and pulling with all their
might, tore him from the wall and the floor.   But
if they did, he left all the skin of his back from
his head to his heels on the floor and the wall
behind him.   But when they were going home
through the hills of Tralee, they found a sheep
on the way, killed it, and clapped the skin on
Conán.   The sheepskin grew to his body; and he
was so well and strong that they sheared him every
year, and got wool enough from his back to make
flannel and frieze for the Fenians of Erin ever
after.

CUCÚLIN.

THERE was a king in a land not far from Greece who had two daughters, and the younger was fairer than the elder daughter.

This old king made a match between the king of Greece and his own elder daughter; but he kept the younger one hidden away till after the marriage. Then the younger daughter came forth to view; and when the king of Greece saw her, he would n't look at his own wife. Nothing would do him but to get the younger sister and leave the elder at home with her father.

The king would n't listen to this, would n't agree to the change, so the king of Greece left his wife where she was, went home alone in a terrible rage and collected all his forces to march against the kingdom of his father-in-law.

He soon conquered the king and his army and, so far as he was able, he vexed and tormented him. To do this the more completely, he took from him a rod of Druidic spells, enchantment, and ring of youth which he had, and, striking the elder sister with the rod, he said: "You will be a serpent of the sea and live outside there in the bay by the castle."

Then turning to the younger sister, whose name was Gil an Og, he struck her, and said: "You 'll be a cat while inside this castle, and have your own form only when you are outside the walls."

After he had done this, the king of Greece went home to his own country, taking with him the rod of enchantment and the ring of youth.

The king died in misery and grief, leaving his two daughters spellbound.

Now there was a Druid in that kingdom, and the younger sister went to consult him, and asked: " Shall I ever be released from the enchantment that's on me now? "

" You will not, unless you find the man to release you; and there is no man in the world to do that but a champion who is now with Fin Mac-Cumhail in Erin."

" Well, how can I find that man? " asked she.

" I will tell you," said the Druid. " Do you make a shirt out of your own hair, take it with you; and never stop till you land in Erin and find Fin and his men; the man that the shirt will fit is the man who will release you."

She began to make the shirt and worked without stopping till it was finished. Then she went on her journey and never rested till she came to Erin in a ship. She went on shore and inquired where Fin and his men were to be found at that time of the year.

" You will find them at Knock an Ar," was the answer she got.

She went to Knock an Ar carrying the shirt with her. The first man she met was Conan Maol, and she said to him: " I have come to find the man this shirt will fit. From the time one man tries it all must try till I see the man it fits."

The shirt went from hand to hand till Cucúlin put it on. " Well," said she, " it fits as your own skin."

Now Gil an Og told Cucúlin all that had happened, — how her father had forced her sister to marry the king of Greece, how this king had made war on her father, enchanted her sister and herself, and carried off the rod of enchantment with the ring of youth, and how the old Druid said the man this shirt would fit was the only man in the world who could release them.

Now Gil an Og and Cucúlin went to the ship and sailed across the seas to her country and went to her castle.

"You 'll have no one but a cat for company to-night," said Gil an Og. " I have the form of a cat inside this castle, but outside I have my own appearance. Your dinner is ready, go in."

After the dinner Cucúlin went to another room apart, and lay down to rest after the journey. The cat came to his pillow, sat there and purred till he fell asleep and slept soundly till morning.

When he rose up, a basin of water, and everything he needed was before him, and his breakfast ready. He walked out after breakfast; Gil an Og was on the green outside before him and said:

" If you are not willing to free my sister and myself, I shall not urge you; but if you do free us, I shall be glad and thankful. Many king's sons and champions before you have gone to recover the ring and the rod; but they have never come back."

"Well, whether I thrive or not, I 'll venture," said Cucúlin.

" I will give you," said Gil an Og, " a present such as I have never given before to any man who ventured out on my behalf; I will give you the speckled boat."

Cucúlin took leave of Gil an Og and sailed away in the speckled boat to Greece, where he went to the king's court, and challenged him to combat.

The king of Greece gathered his forces and sent them out to chastise Cucúlin. He killed them all to the last man. Then Cucúlin challenged the king a second time.

" I have no one now to fight but myself," said the king; " and I don't think it becomes me to go out and meet the like of you."

" If you don't come out to me," said Cucúlin, " I 'll go in to you and cut the head off you in your own castle."

" That 's enough of impudence from you, you scoundrel," said the king of Greece. " I won't have you come into my castle, but I 'll meet you on the open plain."

The king went out, and they fought till Cucúlin got the better of him, bound him head and heels, and said: " I 'll cut the head off you now unless you give me the ring of youth and the rod of enchantment that you took from the father of Gil an Og."

" Well, I did carry them away," said the king, " but it would n't be easy for me now to give them to you or to her; for there was a man who came and carried them away, who could take them from you and from me, and from as many more of us, if they were here."

" Who was that man? " asked Cucúlin.

" His name," said the king, " is Lug [1] Longhand. And if I had known what you wanted, there would have been no difference between us. I 'll tell you how I lost the ring and rod and I 'll go with you and show you where Lug Longhand lives. But do you come to my castle. We 'll have a good time together."

They set out next day, and never stopped till they came opposite Lug Longhand castle, and Cucúlin challenged his forces to combat.

" I have no forces," said Lug, " but I 'll fight

---

[1] Pronounced "Loog."

you myself." So the combat began, and they spent the whole day at one another, and neither gained the victory.

The king of Greece himself put up a tent on the green in front of the castle, and prepared everything necessary to eat and drink (there was no one else to do it). After breakfast next day, Cucúlin and Lug began fighting again. The king of Greece looked on as the day before.

They fought the whole day till near evening, when Cucúlin got the upper hand of Lug Long-hand and bound him head and heels, saying: "I'll cut the head off you now unless you give me the rod and the ring that you carried away from the king of Greece."

"Oh, then," said Lug, "it would be hard for me to give them to you or to him; for forces came and took them from me; and they would have taken them from you and from him, if you had been here."

"Who in the world took them from you?" asked the king of Greece.

"Release me from this bond, and come to my castle, and I'll tell you the whole story," said Lug Longhand.

Cucúlin released him, and they went to the castle. They got good reception and entertainment from Lug that night, and the following morning as well. He said: "The ring and the rod were taken from me by the knight of the island of the Flood. This island is surrounded by a chain, and there is a ring of fire seven miles wide between the chain and the castle. No man can come near the island without breaking the chain, and the moment the chain is broken the fire stops burning at that place; and the instant the fire goes down the knight rushes out and attacks and slays every man that's before him."

The king of Greece, Cucúlin, and Lug Longhand now sailed on in the speckled boat towards the island of the Flood. On the following morning when the speckled boat struck the chain, she was thrown back three days' sail, and was near being sunk, and would have gone to the bottom of the sea but for her own goodness and strength.

As soon as Cucúlin saw what had happened, he took the oars, rowed on again, and drove the vessel forward with such venom that she cut through the chain and went one third of her length on to dry land. That moment the fire was quenched where the vessel struck, and when the knight of the Island saw the fire go out, he rushed to the shore and met Cucúlin, the king of Greece, and Lug Longhand.

When Cucúlin saw him, he threw aside his weapons, caught him, raised him above his head, hurled him down on the flat of his back, bound him head and heels, and said: "I'll cut the head off you unless you give me the ring and the rod that you carried away from Lug Longhand."

"I took them from him, it's true," said the knight; "but it would be hard for me to give them to you now; for a man came and took them from me, who would have taken them from you and all that are with you, and as many more if they had been here before him."

"Who in the world could that man be?" asked Cucúlin.

"The dark Gruagach of the Northern Island. Release me, and come to my castle. I'll tell you all and entertain you well."

He took them to his castle, gave them good cheer, and told them all about the Gruagach and his island. Next morning all sailed away in Cucúlin's vessel, which they had left at the shore of the island, and never stopped till they came to the Gruagach's castle, and pitched their tents in front of it.

Then Cucúlin challenged the Gruagach. The others followed after to know would he thrive. The Gruagach came out and faced Cucúlin, and they began and spent the whole day at one another and neither of them gained the upper hand. When evening came, they stopped and prepared for supper and the night.

Next day after breakfast Cucúlin challenged the Gruagach again, and they fought till evening; when Cucúlin got the better in the struggle, disarmed the Gruagach, bound him, and said: " Unless you give up the rod of enchantment and the ring of youth that you took from the knight of the island of the Flood, I 'll cut the head off you now."

" I took them from him, 't is true; but there was a man named Thin-in-Iron, who took them from me, and he would have taken them from you and from me, and all that are here, if there were twice as many. He is such a man that sword cannot cut him, fire cannot burn him, water cannot drown him, and 't is no easy thing to get the better of him. But if you 'll free me now and come to my castle, I 'll treat you well and tell you all about him." Cucúlin agreed to this.

Next morning they would not stop nor be satisfied till they went their way. They found the castle of Thin-in-Iron, and Cucúlin challenged him to combat. They fought; and he was cutting the flesh from Cucúlin, but Cucúlin's sword cut no flesh from him. They fought till Cucúlin said: " It is time now to stop till to-morrow."

Cucúlin was scarcely able to reach the tent.

They had to support him and put him to bed. Now, who should come to Cucúlin that night but Gil an Og, and she said: "You have gone further than any man before you, and I'll cure you now, and you need go no further for the rod of enchantment and the ring of youth."

"Well," said Cucúlin, "I'll never give over till I knock another day's trial out of Thin-in-Iron."

When it was time for rest, Gil an Og went away, and Cucúlin fell asleep for himself. On the following morning all his comrades were up and facing his tent. They thought to see him dead, but he was in as good health as ever.

They prepared breakfast, and after breakfast Cucúlin went before the door of the castle to challenge his enemy.

Thin-in-Iron thrust his head out and said: "That man I fought yesterday has come again to-day. It would have been a good deed if I had cut the head off him last night. Then he wouldn't be here to trouble me this morning. I won't come home this day till I bring his head with me. Then I'll have peace."

They met in combat and fought till the night was coming. Then Thin-in-Iron cried out for a cessation, and if he did, Cucúlin was glad to give it; for his sword had no effect upon Thin-in-Iron except to tire and nearly kill him (he was enchanted and no arms could cut him). When Thin-in-Iron went to his castle, he threw up three sups of blood, and said to his housekeeper: "Though his sword could not penetrate me, he has nearly broken my heart."

Cucúlin had to be carried to his tent. His comrades laid him on his bed and said: "Whoever came and healed him yesterday, may be the same will be here to-night." They went away and were

not long gone when Gil an Og came and said:
" Cucúlin, if you had done my bidding, you
would n't be as you are to-night.   But if you neglect
my words now, you 'll never see my face again.
I 'll cure you this time and make you as well as
ever ; " and whatever virtue she had she healed him
so he was as strong as before.

" Oh, then," said Cucúlin, " whatever comes on
me I 'll never turn back till I knock another day's
trial out of Thin-in-Iron."

" Well," said she, " you are a stronger man than
he, but there is no good in working at him with a
sword.   Throw your sword aside to-morrow, and
you 'll get the better of him and bind him.   You 'll
not see me again."

She went away and he fell asleep.   His comrades came in the morning and found him sleeping.
They got breakfast, and, after eating, Cucúlin went
out and called a challenge.

" Oh, 't is the same man as yesterday," said
Thin-in-Iron, " and if I had cut the head off him
then, it would n't be he that would trouble me
to-day.   If I live for it, I·'ll bring his head in my
hand to-night, and he 'll never disturb me again."

When Cucúlin saw Thin-in-Iron coming, he
threw his sword aside, and facing him, caught him
by the body, raised him up, then dashed him to
the ground, and said, " If you don't give me what I
want, I 'll cut the head off you."

" What do you want of me ? " asked Thin-in-Iron.

" I want the rod of enchantment and the ring of
youth you carried from the Gruagach."

" I did indeed carry them from him, but it would
be no easy thing for me to give them to you or
any other man ; for a force came which took them
from me."

"What could take them from you?" asked Cucúlin.

"The queen of the Wilderness, an old hag that has them now. But release me from this bondage and I'll take you to my castle and entertain you well, and I'll go with you and the rest of the company to see how will you thrive."

So he took Cucúlin and his friends to the castle and entertained them joyously, and he said: "The old hag, the queen of the Wilderness, lives in a round tower, which is always turning on wheels. There is but one entrance to the tower, and that high above the ground, and in the one chamber in which she lives, keeping the ring and the rod, is a chair, and she has but to sit on the chair and wish herself in any part of the world, and that moment she is there. She has six lines of guards protecting her tower, and if you pass all of these, you'll do what no man before you has done to this day. The first guards are two lions that rush out to know which of them will get the first bite out of the throat of any one that tries to pass. The second are seven men with iron hurlies and an iron ball, and with their hurlies they wallop the life out of any man that goes their way. The third is Hung-up-Naked, who hangs on a tree with his toes to the earth, his head cut from his shoulders and lying on the ground, and who kills every man who comes near him. The fourth is the bull of the Mist that darkens the woods for seven miles around, and destroys everything that enters the Mist. The fifth are seven cats with poison tails; and one drop of their poison would kill the strongest man."

Next morning all went with Cucúlin as far as the lions who guarded the queen of the Wilderness,

an old hag made young by the ring of youth.
The two lions ran at Cucúlin to see which would
have the first bite out of him.

Cucúlin wore a red silk scarf around his neck
and had a fine head of hair. He cut the hair off
his head and wound it around one hand, took his
scarf and wrapped it around the other. Then rushing at the lions, he thrust a hand down the throat
of each lion (for lions can bite neither silk nor
hair). He pulled the livers and lights out of the
two and they fell dead before him. His comrades
looking on, said: " You 'll thrive now since you
have done this deed; " and they left him and went
home, each to his own country.

Cucúlin went further. The next people he met
were the seven men with the iron hurlies (ball
clubs), and they said; " 'T is long since any man
walked this way to us; we 'll have sport now."

The first one said: " Give him a touch of the
hurly and let the others do the same; and we 'll
wallop him till he is dead."

Now Cucúlin drew his sword and cut the head
off the first man before he could make an offer of
the hurly at him; and then he did the same to the
other six.

He went on his way till he came to Hung-up-
Naked, who was hanging from a tree, his head on
the ground near him. The queen of the Wilderness
had fastened him to the tree because he would n't
marry her; and she said: " If any man comes who
will put your head on you, you 'll be free." And
she laid the injunction on him to kill every man
who tried to pass his way without putting the
head on him.

Cucúlin went up, looked at him, and saw heaps

of bones around the tree. The body said: " You
can't go by here. I fight with every man who tries
to pass."

" Well, I 'm not going to fight with a man unless
he has a head on him. Take your head." And
Cucúlin, picking up the head, clapped it on the
body, and said, " Now I 'll fight with you ! "

The man said: " I 'm all right now. I know
where you are going. I 'll stay here till you come;
if you conquer you 'll not forget me. Take the
head off me now; put it where you found it; and
if you succeed, remember that I shall be here
before you on your way home."

Cucúlin went on, but soon met the bull of the
Mist that covered seven miles of the wood with
thick mist. When the bull saw him, he made at
him and stuck a horn in his ribs and threw him
three miles into the wood, against a great oak
tree and broke three ribs in his side.

" Well," said Cucúlin, when he recovered, " if I
get another throw like that, I 'll not be good for
much exercise." He was barely on his feet when
the bull was at him again; but when he came up
he caught the bull by both horns and away they
went wrestling and struggling. For three days
and nights Cucúlin kept the bull in play, till the
morning of the fourth day, when he put him on
the flat of his back. Then he turned him on the
side, and putting a foot on one horn and taking the
other in his two hands, he said: " 'T is well I earned
you; there is not a stitch on me that is n't torn to
rags from wrestling with you." He pulled the
bull asunder from his horns to his tail, into two
equal parts, and said: " Now that I have you in
two, it 's in quarters I 'll put you." He took his

sword, and when he struck the backbone of the bull, the sword remained in the bone and he could n't pull it out.

He walked away and stood awhile and looked. " 'T is hard to say," said he, " that any good champion would leave his sword behind him." So he went back and made another pull and took the hilt off his sword, leaving the blade in the back of the bull. Then he went away tattered and torn, the hilt in his hand, and he turned up towards the forge of the Strong Smith. One of the Smith's boys was out for coal at the time: he saw Cucúlin coming with the hilt in his hand, and ran in, saying: " There is a man coming up and he looks like a fool; we 'll have fun ! "

" Hold your tongue ! " said the master. " Have you heard any account of the bull of the Mist these three days? "

" We have not," said the boys.

" Perhaps," said the Strong Smith, " that 's a good champion that 's coming, and do you mind yourselves."

At that moment Cucúlin walked in to the forge where twelve boys and the master were working. He saluted them and asked, " Can you put a blade in this hilt? "

" We can," said the master. They put in the blade. Cucúlin raised the sword and took a shake out of it and broke it to bits.

"'This is a rotten blade," said he. " Go at it again."

They made a second blade. The boys were in dread of him now. He broke the second blade in the same way as the first. They made six blades, one stronger than the other. He did the same to them all.

"There is no use in talking," said the Strong Smith; "we have no stuff that would make a right blade for you. Go down now," said he to two of the boys, "and bring up an old sword that's down in the stable full of rust."

They went and brought up the sword on two hand-spikes between them; it was so heavy that one couldn't carry it. They gave it to Cucúlin, and with one blow on his heel he knocked the dust from it and went out at the door and took a shake out of it; and if he did, he darkened the whole place with the rust from the blade.

"This is my sword, whoever made it," said he.

"It is," said the master; "it's yours and welcome. I know who you are now, and where you are going. Remember that I'm in bondage here." The Strong Smith took Cucúlin then to his house, gave him refreshment and clothes for the journey. When he was ready, the Smith said: "I hope you'll thrive. You have done a deal more than any man that ever walked this way before. There is nothing now to stand in your way till you come to the seven cats outside the turning tower. If they shake their tails and a drop of poison comes on you, it will penetrate to your heart. You must sweep off their tails with your sword. 'T is equal to you what their bodies will do after that."

Cucúlin soon came to them and there wasn't one of the seven cats he didn't strip of her tail before she knew he was in it. He cared nothing for the bodies so he had the tails. The cats ran away.

Now he faced the tower turning on wheels. The queen of the Wilderness was in it. He had been told by Thin-in-Iron that he must cut the axle. He found the axle, cut it, and the tower stopped that instant.   Cucúlin made a spring and went in through the single passage.

The old hag was preparing to sit on the chair as she saw him coming.   He sprang forward, pushed the chair away with one hand, and, catching her by the back of the neck with the other, said: " You are to lose your head now, old woman! "

" Spare me, and what you want you'll get," said she.   " I have the ring of youth and the rod of enchantment," and she gave them to him.   He put the ring on his finger, and saying, " You'll never do mischief again to man! " he turned her face to the entrance, and gave her a kick.   Out she flew through the opening and down to the ground, where she broke her neck and died on the spot.

Cucúlin made the Strong Smith king over all the dominions of the queen of the Wilderness, and proclaimed that any person in the country who refused to obey the new king would be put to death.

Cucúlin turned back at once, and travelled till he came to Hung-up-Naked.   He took him down and, putting the head on his body, struck him a blow of the rod and made the finest looking man of him that could be found.   The man went back to his own home happy and well.

Cucúlin never stopped till he came to the castle of Gil an Og.   She was outside with a fine welcome before him; and why not, to be sure, for he had the rod of enchantment and the ring of youth!

When she entered the castle and took the form of a cat, he struck her a blow of the rod and she gained the same form and face she had before the king of Greece struck her.   Then he asked, " Where is your sister? "

" In the lake there outside," answered Gil an Og, " in the form of a sea-serpent." She went out with him, and the moment they came to the edge of the lake the sister rose up near them. Then Cucúlin struck her with the rod and she came to land in her own shape and countenance.

Next day they saw a deal of vessels facing the harbor, and what should they be but a fleet of ships, and on the ships were the king of Greece, Lug Longhand, the knight of the island of the Flood, the Dark Grúagach of the Northern Island and Thin-in-Iron: and they came each in his own vessel to know was there any account of Cucúlin. There was good welcome for them all, and when they had feasted and rejoiced together Cucúlin married Gil an Og. The king of Greece took Gil an Og's sister, who was his own wife at first, and went home.

Cucúlin went away himself with his wife Gil an Og, never stopping till he came to Erin; and when he came, Fin MacCumhail and his men were at KilConaly, near the river Shannon.

When Cucúlin went from Erin he left a son whose mother was called the Virago of Alba: she was still alive and the son was eighteen years old. When she heard that Cucúlin had brought Gil an Og to Erin, she was enraged with jealousy and madness. She had reared the son, whose name was Conlán, like any king's son, and now giving him his arms of a champion she told him to go to his father.

" I would," said he, " if I knew who my father is."

" His name is Cucúlin, and he is with Fin MacCumhail. I bind you not to yield to any man," said she to her son, " nor tell your name to any man till you fight him out."

Conlán started from Ulster where his mother

was, and never stopped till he was facing Fin and
his men, who were hunting that day along the
cliffs of KilConaly.

When the young man came up Fin said, "There
is a single man facing us."

Conan Maol said, "Let some one go against
him, ask who he is and what he wants."

"I never give an account of myself to any man,"
said Conlán, "till I get an account from him."

"There is no man among us," said Conan,
"bound in that way but Cucúlin." They called on
Cucúlin; he came up and the two fought. Conlán
knew by the description his mother had given that
Cucúlin was his father, but Cucúlin did not know
his son. Every time Conlán aimed his spear he
threw it so as to strike the ground in front of
Cucúlin's toe, but Cucúlin aimed straight at him.

They were at one another three days and three
nights. The son always sparing the father, the
father never sparing the son.

Conan Maol came to them the fourth morning.
"Cucúlin," said he, "I did n't expect to see any
man standing against you three days, and you such
a champion."

When Conlán heard Conan Maol urging the
father to kill him, he gave a bitter look at Conan,
and forgot his guard. Cucúlin's spear went through
his head that minute, and he fell. "I die of that
blow from my father," said he.

"Are you my son?" said Cucúlin.

"I am," said Conlán.

Cucúlin took his sword and cut the head off him
sooner than leave him in the punishment and pain
he was in. Then he faced all the people, and Fin
was looking on.

"There's trouble on Cucúlin," said Fin.

"Chew your thumb," said Conan Maol, "to know what's on him."

Fin chewed his thumb, and said, "Cucúlin is after killing his own son, and if I and all my men were to face him before his passion cools, at the end of seven days, he'd destroy every man of us."

"Go now," said Conan, "and bind him to go down to Bale strand and give seven days' fighting against the waves of the sea, rather than kill us all."

So Fin bound him to go down. When he went to Bale strand Cucúlin found a great white stone. He grasped his sword in his right hand and cried out: "If I had the head of the woman who sent her son into peril of death at my hand, I'd split it as I split this stone," and he made four quarters of the stone. Then he strove with the waves seven days and nights till he fell from hunger and weakness, and the waves went over him.

OISIN IN TIR NA N–OG.

THERE was a king in Tir na n-Og (the land of Youth) who held the throne and crown for many a year against all comers; and the law of the kingdom was that every seventh year the champions and best men of the country should run for the office of king.

Once in seven years they all met at the front of the palace and ran to the top of a hill two miles distant. On the top of that hill was a chair and the man that sat first in the chair was king of Tir na n-Og for the next seven years. After he had ruled for ages, the king became anxious; he was afraid that some one might sit in the chair before him, and take the crown off his head. So he called up his Druid one day and asked: " How long shall I keep the chair to rule this land, and will any man sit in it before me and take the crown off my head? "

" You will keep the chair and the crown forever," said the Druid, " unless your own son-in-law takes them from you."

The king had no sons and but one daughter, the finest woman in Tir na n-Og; and the like of her could not be found in Erin or any kingdom in the world. When the king heard the words of the Druid, he said, "I 'll have no son-in-law, for I 'll put the daughter in a way no man will marry her."

Then he took a rod of Druidic spells, and calling the daughter up before him, he struck her with the rod, and put a pig's head on her in place of her own.

Then he sent the daughter away to her own place in the castle, and turning to the Druid said: " There is no man that will marry her now."

When the Druid saw the face that was on the princess with the pig's head that the father gave her, he grew very sorry that he had given such information to the king; and some time after he went to see the princess.

" Must I be in this way forever? " asked she of the Druid.

" You must," said he, " till you marry one of the sons of Fin MacCumhail in Erin. If you marry one of Fin's sons, you 'll be freed from the blot that is on you now, and get back your own head and countenance."

When she heard this she was impatient in her mind, and could never rest till she left Tir na n-Og and came to Erin. When she had inquired she heard that Fin and the Fenians of Erin were at that time living on Knock an Ar, and she made her way to the place without delay and lived there a while; and when she saw Oisin, he pleased her; and when she found out that he was a son of Fin MacCumhail, she was always making up to him and coming towards him. And it was usual for the Fenians in those days to go out hunting on the hills and mountains and in the woods of Erin, and when one of them went he always took five or six men with him to bring home the game.

On a day Oisin set out with his men and dogs to the woods; and he went so far and killed so much game that when it was brought together, the men were so tired, weak, and hungry that they could n't carry it, but went away home and left him with the three dogs, Bran, Sciolán, and Buglén,[1] to shift for himself.

[1] Celebrated dogs of Fin MacCumhail.

Now the daughter of the king of Tir na n-Og, who was herself the queen of Youth, followed closely in the hunt all that day, and when the men left Oisin she came up to him; and as he stood looking at the great pile of game and said, " I am very sorry to leave behind anything that I 've had the trouble of killing," she looked at him and said, " Tie up a bundle for me, and I 'll carry it to lighten the load off you."

Oisin gave her a bundle of the game to carry, and took the remainder himself. The evening was very warm and the game heavy, and after they had gone some distance, Oisin said, " Let us rest a while." Both threw down their burdens, and put their backs against a great stone that was by the roadside. The woman was heated and out of breath, and opened her dress to cool herself. Then Oisin looked at her and saw her beautiful form and her white bosom.

"Oh, then," said he, " it 's a pity you have the pig's head on you; for I have never seen such an appearance on a woman in all my life before."

" Well," said she, " my father is the king of Tir na n-Og, and I was the finest woman in his kingdom and the most beautiful of all, till he put me under a Druidic spell and gave me the pig's head that 's on me now in place of my own. And the Druid of Tir na n-Og came to me afterwards, and told me that if one of the sons of Fin Mac-Cumhail would marry me, the pig's head would vanish, and I should get back my face in the same form as it was before my father struck me with the Druid's wand. When I heard this I never stopped till I came to Erin, where I found your father and picked you out among the sons of Fin MacCumhail, and followed you to see would you marry me and set me free."

"If that is the state you are in, and if marriage with me will free you from the spell, I'll not leave the pig's head on you long."

So they got married without delay, not waiting to take home the game or to lift it from the ground. That moment the pig's head was gone, and the king's daughter had the same face and beauty that she had before her father struck her with the Druidic wand.

"Now," said the queen of Youth to Oisin, "I cannot stay here long, and unless you come with me to Tir na n-Og we must part."

"Oh," said Oisin, "wherever you go I'll go, and wherever you turn I'll follow."

Then she turned and Oisin went with her, not going back to Knock an Ar to see his father or his son. That very day they set out for Tir na n-Og and never stopped till they came to her father's castle; and when they came, there was a welcome before them, for the king thought his daughter was lost. That same year there was to be a choice of a king, and when the appointed day came at the end of the seventh year all the great men and the champions, and the king himself, met together at the front of the castle to run and see who should be first in the chair on the hill; but before a man of them was half way to the hill, Oisin was sitting above in the chair before them. After that time no one stood up to run for the office against Oisin, and he spent many a happy year as king in Tir na n-Og. At last he said to his wife: "I wish I could be in Erin to-day to see my father and his men."

"If you go," said his wife, "and set foot on the land of Erin, you'll never come back here to me, and you'll become a blind old man. How long do you think it is since you came here?"

"About three years," said Oisin.

" It is three hundred years," said she, " since you came to this kingdom with me. If you must go to Erin, I 'll give you this white steed to carry you ; but if you come down from the steed or touch the soil of Erin with your foot, the steed will come back that minute, and you 'll be where he left you, a poor old man."

" I 'll come back, never fear," said Oisin. " Have I not good reason to come back? But I must see my father and my son and my friends in Erin once more ; I must have even one look at them."

She prepared the steed for Oisin and said, " This steed will carry you wherever you wish to go."

Oisin never stopped till the steed touched the soil of Erin ; and he went on till he came to Knock Patrick in Munster, where he saw a man herding cows. In the field, where the cows were grazing there was a broad flat stone.

" Will you come here," said Oisin to the herdsman, " and turn over this stone? "

" Indeed, then, I will not," said the herdsman ; " for I could not lift it, nor twenty men more like me."

Oisin rode up to the stone, and, reaching down, caught it with his hand and turned it over. Underneath the stone was the great horn of the Fenians (*borabu*), which circled round like a seashell, and it was the rule that when any of the Fenians of Erin blew the borabu, the others would assemble at once from whatever part of the country they might be in at the time.

" Will you bring this horn to me ! " asked Oisin of the herdsman.

" I will not," said the herdsman ; " for neither I nor many more like me could raise it from the ground."

With that Oisin moved near the horn, and reaching down took it in his hand; but so eager was he to blow it, that he forgot everything, and slipped in reaching till one foot touched the earth. In an instant the steed was gone, and Oisin lay on the ground a blind old man. The herdsman went to Saint Patrick, who lived near by, and told him what had happened.

Saint Patrick sent a man and a horse for Oisin, brought him to his own house, gave him a room by himself, and sent a boy to stay with him to serve and take care of him. And Saint Patrick commanded his cook to send Oisin plenty of meat and drink, to give him bread and beef and butter every day.

Now Oisin lived a while in this way. The cook sent him provisions each day, and Saint Patrick himself asked him all kinds of questions about the old times of the Fenians of Erin. Oisin told him about his father, Fin MacCumhail, about himself, his son Osgar, Goll MacMorna, Conan Maol, Diarmuid, and all the Fenian heroes; how they fought, feasted, and hunted, how they came under Druidic spells, and how they were freed from them.

At the same time, Saint Patrick was putting up a great building; but what his men used to put up in the daytime was levelled at night, and Saint Patrick lamented over his losses in the hearing of Oisin. Then Oisin said in the hearing of Saint Patrick, " If I had my strength and my sight, I 'd put a stop to the power that is levelling your work."

" Do you think you 'd be able to do that," said Saint Patrick, " and let my building go on? "

" I do, indeed," said Oisin.

So Saint Patrick prayed to the Lord, and the sight and strength came back to Oisin. He went to the woods and got a great club and stood at the building on guard.

What should come in the night but a great beast in the form of a bull, which began to uproot and destroy the work. But if he did Oisin faced him, and the battle began hot and heavy between the two; but in the course of the night Oisin got the upper hand of the bull and left him dead before the building. Then he stretched out on the ground himself and fell asleep.

Now Saint Patrick was waiting at home to know how would the battle come out, and thinking Oisin too long away he sent a messenger to the building; and when the messenger came he saw the ground torn up, a hill in one place and a hollow in the next. The bull was dead and Oisin sleeping after the desperate battle. He went back and told what he saw.

"Oh," said Saint Patrick, "it's better to knock the strength out of him again; for he'll kill us all if he gets vexed."

Saint Patrick took the strength out of him, and when Oisin woke up he was a blind old man and the messenger went out and brought him home.

Oisin lived on for a time as before. The cook sent him his food, the boy served him, and Saint Patrick listened to the stories of the Fenians of Erin.

Saint Patrick had a neighbor, a Jew, a very rich man but the greatest miser in the kingdom, and he had the finest haggart of corn in Erin. Well, the Jew and Saint Patrick got very intimate with one another and so great became the friendship of the Jew for Saint Patrick at last, that he said he'd give him, for the support of his house, as much corn as one man could thrash out of the haggart[1] in a day.

When Saint Patrick went home after getting the promise of the corn, he told in the hearing of Oisin about what the Jew had said.

"Oh, then," said Oisin, "if I had my sight and strength, I'd thrash as much corn in one day as would do · your whole house for a twelvemonth and more."

"Will you do that for me?" said Saint Patrick.

"I will," said Oisin.

Saint Patrick prayed again to the Lord, and the sight and strength came back to Oisin. He went to the woods next morning at daybreak, Oisin did, pulled up two fine ash-trees and made a flail of them. After eating his breakfast he left the house and never stopped till he faced the haggart of the Jew. Standing before one of the stacks of wheat he hit it a wallop of his flail and broke it asunder. He kept on in this way till he slashed the whole haggart to and fro, — and the Jew running like mad up and down the highroad in front of the haggart, tearing the hair from his head when he saw what was doing to his wheat, and the face gone from him entirely he was so in dread of Oisin.

When the haggart was thrashed clean, Oisin went to Saint Patrick and told him to send his men for the wheat; for he had thrashed out the whole haggart. When Saint Patrick saw the countenance that was on Oisin, and heard what he had done he was greatly in dread of him, and knocked the strength out of him again, and Oisin became an old, blind man as before.

Saint Patrick's men went to the haggart and

[1] Haggart, hay-yard.

there was so much wheat they did n't bring the half of it away with them and they did n't want it.

Oisin again lived for a while as before and then he was vexed because the cook did n't give him what he wanted. He told Saint Patrick that he was n't getting enough to eat. Then Saint Patrick called up the cook before himself and Oisin and asked her what she was giving Oisin to eat. She said: " I give him at every meal what bread is baked on a large griddle and all the butter I make in one churn, and a quarter of beef besides."

" That ought to be enough for you," said Saint Patrick.

" Oh, then," said Oisin, turning to the cook, " I have often seen the leg of a blackbird bigger than the quarter of beef you give me, I have often seen an ivy leaf bigger than the griddle on which you bake the bread for me, and I have often seen a single rowan berry [the mountain ash berry] bigger than the bit of butter you give me to eat."

" You lie ! " said the cook, " you never did."

Oisin said not a word in answer.

Now there was a hound in the place that was going to have her first whelps, and Oisin said to the boy who was tending him: " Do you mind and get the first whelp she 'll have and drown the others."

Next morning the boy found three whelps, and coming back to Oisin, said: " There are three whelps and 't is unknown which of them is the first."

At Saint Patrick's house they had slaughtered an ox the day before, and Oisin said: " Go now and bring the hide of the ox and hang it up in this room." When the hide was hung up Oisin

said, " Bring here the three whelps and throw
them up against the hide." The boy threw up
one of the whelps against the oxhide. " What
did he do? " asked Oisin.

" What did he do," said the boy, " but fall to
the ground."

" Throw up another," said Oisin. The boy
threw another. " What did he do? " asked Oisin.

" What did he do but to fall the same as the
first."

The third whelp was thrown and he held fast to
the hide, — did n't fall. " What did he do? "
asked Oisin.

" Oh," said the boy, " he kept his hold."

" Take him down," said Oisin; " give him to
the mother: bring both in here; feed the mother
well and drown the other two."

The boy did as he was commanded, and fed the
two well, and when the whelp grew up the mother
was banished, the whelp chained up and fed for
a year and a day. And when the year and a day
were spent, Oisin said, " We'll go hunting to-
morrow, and we'll take the dog with us."

They went next day, the boy guiding Oisin,
holding the dog by a chain. They went first to
the place where Oisin had touched earth and lost
the magic steed from Tir na n-Og. The borabu
of the Fenians of Erin was lying on the ground
there still. Oisin took it up and they went on to
Glen na Smuil (Thrushs's Glen). When at the
edge of the glen Oisin began to sound the borabu.
Birds and beasts of every kind came hurrying
forward. He blew the horn till the glen was full
of them from end to end.

" What do you see now? " asked he of the boy.

" The glen is full of living things."

" What is the dog doing? "

" He is looking ahead and his hair is on end."

" Do you see anything else? "

" I see a great bird all black settling down on the north side of the glen."

" That's what I want," said Oisin; " what is the dog doing now? "

" Oh, the eyes are coming out of his head, and there is n't a rib of hair on his body that is n't standing up."

" Let him go now," said Oisin. The boy let slip the chain and the dog rushed through the glen killing everything before him.   When all the others were dead he turned to the great blackbird and killed that.   Then he faced Oisin and the boy and came bounding toward them with venom and fierceness.   Oisin drew out of his bosom a brass ball and said: " If you don't throw this into the dog's mouth he 'll destroy us both; knock the dog with the ball or he 'll tear us to pieces."

" Oh," said the boy, " I 'll never be able to throw the ball, I 'm so in dread of the dog."

" Come here at my back, then," said Oisin, " and straighten my hand towards the dog."   The boy directed the hand and Oisin threw the ball into the dog's mouth and killed him on the spot.

" What have we done? " asked Oisin.

" Oh, the dog is knocked," said the boy.

" We are all right then," said Oisin, " and do you lead me now to the blackbird of the carn, I don't care for the others."

They went to the great bird, kindled a fire and cooked all except one of its legs.   Then Oisin ate as much as he wanted and said; " I 've had a good meal of my own hunting and it 's many and many a day since I have had one.   Now let us go on farther."

They went into the woods, and soon Oisin asked the boy; " Do you see anything wonderful? "

" I see an ivy with the largest leaves I have ever set eyes on."

" Take one leaf of that ivy," said Oisin.

The boy took the leaf. Near the ivy they found a rowan berry, and then went home taking the three things with them, — the blackbird's leg, the ivy leaf, and the rowan berry. When they reached the house Oisin called for the cook, and Saint Patrick made her come to the fore. When she came Oisin pointed to the blackbird's leg and asked, " Which is larger, that leg or the quarter of beef you give me? "

" Oh, that is a deal larger," said the cook.

" You were right in that case," said Saint Patrick to Oisin.

Then Oisin drew out the ivy leaf and asked, " Which is larger, this or the griddle on which you made bread for me? "

" That is larger than the griddle and the bread together," said the cook.

" Right again," said Saint Patrick.

Oisin now took out the rowan berry and asked: " Which is larger, this berry or the butter of one churning which you give me? "

" Oh, that is bigger," said the cook, " than both the churn and the butter."

" Right, every time," said Saint Patrick.

Then Oisin raised his arm and swept the head off the cook with a stroke from the edge of his hand, saying, " You'll never give the lie to an honest man again."

NOTES.

Aedh Curucha (*Aedh Crochtha*), Hugh, the "suspended" or "hung up." As Aedh means also a fire-spark as well as the modern name Hugh, Aedh Curucha means the hung up or suspended fire-spark.

Alba, former name of Scotland.

Bar an Súan, "pin of slumber," met with frequently in Gaelic mythology, is found among the Slavs, but not so often. It appears in a Russian story, — one of the most beautiful in European folk-lore.

Cesa MacRi na Tulach, "Cesa, son of the king of the hill," said by my Donegal informant to be a small dark-gray bird.

Cúrucha na Gros (*Crochtha na g-cros*), "hung on the crosses," is a very interesting name, as is also that of the father of Fair, Brown, and Trembling, Aedh Curucha, *q. v.*

Conán Maol MacMorna, the Gaelic Thersites, always railing, causing trouble, unpopular, and attracting attention. This species of person is as well known in the mythology of the North American Indians as in Aryan myths.

Diachbha (pronounced Dyeéachva), "divinity," or the working of a power outside of us in shaping the careers of men ; fate.

Diarmuid (pronounced Dyeearmud), the final *d* sounded as if one were to begin to utter *y* after it), one of the most remarkable characters in Gaelic mythology, a great hunter and performer of marvellous feats. The prominent event of his life was the carrying off of Grainne, bride of Fin MacCumhail, at her own command. After many years of baffled pursuit, Fin was forced to make peace ; but he contrived at last to bring about Diarmuid's death by causing him to hunt an enchanted boar of green color and without ears or tail. The account of this pursuit and the death of Diarmuid forms one of the celebrated productions of Gaelic literature. Diarmuid had a mole on his forehead, which he kept covered usually ; but when it was laid bare and a woman saw it, she fell in love with him beyond recall. This was why Grainne deserted Fin, not after she was married, but at the feast of betrothal. The evident meaning of the word is "bright" or "divine-weaponed." It is very interesting to find Diarmuid called also Son of the Monarch of Light, in another story.

Donoch Kam cosa, " Donoch, crooked feet."

Draoiachta (pronounced Dreéachta), "Druidism," or "enchantment."

Érineach, or *Eirineach,* "a man of Erin."

Gil an Og, "water of youth."

Gilla na Grakin (*Gilla na g-croicean*), "the fellow (or youth) of the skins," — *i. e.,* the serving man of the skins. This word "Gilla" enters into the formation of many Gaelic names, such as Gilchrist, Gilfillin, MacGillacuddy.

Grúagach (pronounced *Gróoagach*), "the hairy one," from *grúag,* hair. We are more likely to be justified in finding a solar agent concealed in the person of the laughing Gruagach or the Gruagach of tricks than in many of the sun-myths put forth by some modern writers.

Inis Caol, "light island," — *i. e.,* not heavy.

Iron-back-without-action (*Ton iaran gan tapuil*).

Knock an Ár, "hill of slaughter," a mountain near the mouth of the Shannon in Kerry.

Lun Dubh MacSmola, "blackbird," son of thrush.

Mal MacMulcan. Mulcan in this name is evidently Vulcan, substituted for some old Gaelic myth-power.

Oisin. In the Gaelic of Ireland this name is accented on the last syllable ; in that of Scotland on the first, which gives in English Ossian, the poet made known to the world by Macpherson. The poems of Ossian are of course nothing more nor less than the ballads of Fin MacCumhail and the Fenians of Erin, taken from Ireland to Scotland by the Gael when they settled in the latter country, and modified in some degree by Macpherson. Oisin is pronounced Ushéen in Ireland, *u* sounded as in *but*.

Ri Fohín (Ri fo thuinn), "king under the wave."

Sean Ruadh, "John the Red," pronounced Shawn Roo.

Tisean (pronounced *Tishyán ; an* as in *pan*), "envy." Son of King Tisean means "Son of King Envy."

Urféist. This word is made up of *Ur* and *péist*. *Ur* is kindred with the German *Ur*, and in a compound like this means the "original" or "greatest." *Péist* — "worm," "beast," "monster" — is changed to *féist* here, according to a rule of aspiration in Gaelic grammar.

A CATALOG OF SELECTED
DOVER BOOKS
IN ALL FIELDS OF INTEREST

A CATALOG OF SELECTED DOVER
BOOKS IN ALL FIELDS OF INTEREST

DRAWINGS OF REMBRANDT, edited by Seymour Slive. Updated Lippmann, Hofstede de Groot edition, with definitive scholarly apparatus. All portraits, biblical sketches, landscapes, nudes. Oriental figures, classical studies, together with selection of work by followers. 550 illustrations. Total of 630pp. 9⅛ × 12¼.
21485-0, 21486-9 Pa., Two-vol. set $25.00

GHOST AND HORROR STORIES OF AMBROSE BIERCE, Ambrose Bierce. 24 tales vividly imagined, strangely prophetic, and decades ahead of their time in technical skill: "The Damned Thing," "An Inhabitant of Carcosa," "The Eyes of the Panther," "Moxon's Master," and 20 more. 199pp. 5⅜ × 8½. 20767-6 Pa. $3.95

ETHICAL WRITINGS OF MAIMONIDES, Maimonides. Most significant ethical works of great medieval sage, newly translated for utmost precision, readability. Laws Concerning Character Traits, Eight Chapters, more. 192pp. 5⅜ × 8½.
24522-5 Pa. $4.50

THE EXPLORATION OF THE COLORADO RIVER AND ITS CANYONS, J. W. Powell. Full text of Powell's 1,000-mile expedition down the fabled Colorado in 1869. Superb account of terrain, geology, vegetation, Indians, famine, mutiny, treacherous rapids, mighty canyons, during exploration of last unknown part of continental U.S. 400pp. 5⅜ × 8½. 20094-9 Pa. $6.95

HISTORY OF PHILOSOPHY, Julián Marías. Clearest one-volume history on the market. Every major philosopher and dozens of others, to Existentialism and later. 505pp. 5⅜ × 8½. 21739-6 Pa. $8.50

ALL ABOUT LIGHTNING, Martin A. Uman. Highly readable non-technical survey of nature and causes of lightning, thunderstorms, ball lightning, St. Elmo's Fire, much more. Illustrated. 192pp. 5⅜ × 8½. 25237-X Pa. $5.95

SAILING ALONE AROUND THE WORLD, Captain Joshua Slocum. First man to sail around the world, alone, in small boat. One of great feats of seamanship told in delightful manner. 67 illustrations. 294pp. 5⅜ × 8½. 20326-3 Pa. $4.95

LETTERS AND NOTES ON THE MANNERS, CUSTOMS AND CONDITIONS OF THE NORTH AMERICAN INDIANS, George Catlin. Classic account of life among Plains Indians: ceremonies, hunt, warfare, etc. 312 plates. 572pp. of text. 6⅛ × 9¼. 22118-0, 22119-9 Pa. Two-vol. set $15.90

ALASKA: The Harriman Expedition, 1899, John Burroughs, John Muir, et al. Informative, engrossing accounts of two-month, 9,000-mile expedition. Native peoples, wildlife, forests, geography, salmon industry, glaciers, more. Profusely illustrated. 240 black-and-white line drawings. 124 black-and-white photographs. 3 maps. Index. 576pp. 5⅜ × 8½. 25109-8 Pa. $11.95

THE BOOK OF BEASTS: Being a Translation from a Latin Bestiary of the Twelfth Century, T. H. White. Wonderful catalog real and fanciful beasts: manticore, griffin, phoenix, amphivius, jaculus, many more. White's witty erudite commentary on scientific, historical aspects. Fascinating glimpse of medieval mind. Illustrated. 296pp. 5⅜ × 8¼. (Available in U.S. only) 24609-4 Pa. $5.95

FRANK LLOYD WRIGHT: ARCHITECTURE AND NATURE With 160 Illustrations, Donald Hoffmann. Profusely illustrated study of influence of nature—especially prairie—on Wright's designs for Fallingwater, Robie House, Guggenheim Museum, other masterpieces. 96pp. 9¼ × 10¾. 25098-9 Pa. $7.95

FRANK LLOYD WRIGHT'S FALLINGWATER, Donald Hoffmann. Wright's famous waterfall house: planning and construction of organic idea. History of site, owners, Wright's personal involvement. Photographs of various stages of building. Preface by Edgar Kaufmann, Jr. 100 illustrations. 112pp. 9¼ × 10. 23671-4 Pa. $7.95

YEARS WITH FRANK LLOYD WRIGHT: Apprentice to Genius, Edgar Tafel. Insightful memoir by a former apprentice presents a revealing portrait of Wright the man, the inspired teacher, the greatest American architect. 372 black-and-white illustrations. Preface. Index. vi + 228pp. 8¼ × 11. 24801-1 Pa. $9.95

THE STORY OF KING ARTHUR AND HIS KNIGHTS, Howard Pyle. Enchanting version of King Arthur fable has delighted generations with imaginative narratives of exciting adventures and unforgettable illustrations by the author. 41 illustrations. xviii + 313pp. 6⅛ × 9¼. 21445-1 Pa. $5.95

THE GODS OF THE EGYPTIANS, E. A. Wallis Budge. Thorough coverage of numerous gods of ancient Egypt by foremost Egyptologist. Information on evolution of cults, rites and gods; the cult of Osiris; the Book of the Dead and its rites; the sacred animals and birds; Heaven and Hell; and more. 956pp. 6⅛ × 9¼. 22055-9, 22056-7 Pa., Two-vol. set $21.90

A THEOLOGICO-POLITICAL TREATISE, Benedict Spinoza. Also contains unfinished *Political Treatise*. Great classic on religious liberty, theory of government on common consent. R. Elwes translation. Total of 421pp. 5⅜ × 8½. 20249-6 Pa. $6.95

INCIDENTS OF TRAVEL IN CENTRAL AMERICA, CHIAPAS, AND YUCATAN, John L. Stephens. Almost single-handed discovery of Maya culture; exploration of ruined cities, monuments, temples; customs of Indians. 115 drawings. 892pp. 5⅜ × 8½. 22404-X, 22405-8 Pa., Two-vol. set $15.90

LOS CAPRICHOS, Francisco Goya. 80 plates of wild, grotesque monsters and caricatures. Prado manuscript included. 183pp. 6⅝ × 9⅝. 22384-1 Pa. $4.95

AUTOBIOGRAPHY: The Story of My Experiments with Truth, Mohandas K. Gandhi. Not hagiography, but Gandhi in his own words. Boyhood, legal studies, purification, the growth of the Satyagraha (nonviolent protest) movement. Critical, inspiring work of the man who freed India. 480pp. 5⅜ × 8½. (Available in U.S. only) 24593-4 Pa. $6.95

ILLUSTRATED DICTIONARY OF HISTORIC ARCHITECTURE, edited by Cyril M. Harris. Extraordinary compendium of clear, concise definitions for over 5,000 important architectural terms complemented by over 2,000 line drawings. Covers full spectrum of architecture from ancient ruins to 20th-century Modernism. Preface. 592pp. 7½ × 9⅝. 24444-X Pa. $14.95

THE NIGHT BEFORE CHRISTMAS, Clement Moore. Full text, and woodcuts from original 1848 book. Also critical, historical material. 19 illustrations. 40pp. 4⅝ × 6. 22797-9 Pa. $2.50

THE LESSON OF JAPANESE ARCHITECTURE: 165 Photographs, Jiro Harada. Memorable gallery of 165 photographs taken in the 1930's of exquisite Japanese homes of the well-to-do and historic buildings. 13 line diagrams. 192pp. 8⅜ × 11¼. 24778-3 Pa. $8.95

THE AUTOBIOGRAPHY OF CHARLES DARWIN AND SELECTED LET-TERS, edited by Francis Darwin. The fascinating life of eccentric genius composed of an intimate memoir by Darwin (intended for his children); commentary by his son, Francis; hundreds of fragments from notebooks, journals, papers; and letters to and from Lyell, Hooker, Huxley, Wallace and Henslow. xi + 365pp. 5⅜ × 8. 20479-0 Pa. $5.95

WONDERS OF THE SKY: Observing Rainbows, Comets, Eclipses, the Stars and Other Phenomena, Fred Schaaf. Charming, easy-to-read poetic guide to all manner of celestial events visible to the naked eye. Mock suns, glories, Belt of Venus, more. Illustrated. 299pp. 5¼ × 8¼. 24402-4 Pa. $7.95

BURNHAM'S CELESTIAL HANDBOOK, Robert Burnham, Jr. Thorough guide to the stars beyond our solar system. Exhaustive treatment. Alphabetical by constellation: Andromeda to Cetus in Vol. 1; Chamaeleon to Orion in Vol. 2; and Pavo to Vulpecula in Vol. 3. Hundreds of illustrations. Index in Vol. 3. 2,000pp. 6⅛ × 9¼. 23567-X, 23568-8, 23673-0 Pa., Three-vol. set $37.85

STAR NAMES: Their Lore and Meaning, Richard Hinckley Allen. Fascinating history of names various cultures have given to constellations and literary and folkloristic uses that have been made of stars. Indexes to subjects. Arabic and Greek names. Biblical references. Bibliography. 563pp. 5⅜ × 8½. 21079-0 Pa. $7.95

THIRTY YEARS THAT SHOOK PHYSICS: The Story of Quantum Theory, George Gamow. Lucid, accessible introduction to influential theory of energy and matter. Careful explanations of Dirac's anti-particles, Bohr's model of the atom, much more. 12 plates. Numerous drawings. 240pp. 5⅜ × 8½. 24895-X Pa. $4.95

CHINESE DOMESTIC FURNITURE IN PHOTOGRAPHS AND MEASURED DRAWINGS, Gustav Ecke. A rare volume, now affordably priced for antique collectors, furniture buffs and art historians. Detailed review of styles ranging from early Shang to late Ming. Unabridged republication. 161 black-and-white draw-ings, photos. Total of 224pp. 8⅜ × 11¼. (Available in U.S. only) 25171-3 Pa. $12.95

VINCENT VAN GOGH: A Biography, Julius Meier-Graefe. Dynamic, penetrat-ing study of artist's life, relationship with brother, Theo, painting techniques, travels, more. Readable, engrossing. 160pp. 5⅜ × 8½. (Available in U.S. only) 25253-1 Pa. $3.95

HOW TO WRITE, Gertrude Stein. Gertrude Stein claimed anyone could understand her unconventional writing—here are clues to help. Fascinating improvisations, language experiments, explanations illuminate Stein's craft and the art of writing. Total of 414pp. 4⅜ × 6⅜. 23144-5 Pa. $5.95

ADVENTURES AT SEA IN THE GREAT AGE OF SAIL: Five Firsthand Narratives, edited by Elliot Snow. Rare true accounts of exploration, whaling, shipwreck, fierce natives, trade, shipboard life, more. 33 illustrations. Introduction. 353pp. 5⅜ × 8½. 25177-2 Pa. $7.95

THE HERBAL OR GENERAL HISTORY OF PLANTS, John Gerard. Classic descriptions of about 2,850 plants—with over 2,700 illustrations—includes Latin and English names, physical descriptions, varieties, time and place of growth, more. 2,706 illustrations. xlv + 1,678pp. 8½ × 12¼. 23147-X Cloth. $75.00

DOROTHY AND THE WIZARD IN OZ, L. Frank Baum. Dorothy and the Wizard visit the center of the Earth, where people are vegetables, glass houses grow and Oz characters reappear. Classic sequel to *Wizard of Oz*. 256pp. 5⅜ × 8.
24714-7 Pa. $4.95

SONGS OF EXPERIENCE: Facsimile Reproduction with 26 Plates in Full Color, William Blake. This facsimile of Blake's original "Illuminated Book" reproduces 26 full-color plates from a rare 1826 edition. Includes "The Tyger," "London," "Holy Thursday," and other immortal poems. 26 color plates. Printed text of poems. 48pp. 5¼ × 7. 24636-1 Pa. $3.50

SONGS OF INNOCENCE, William Blake. The first and most popular of Blake's famous "Illuminated Books," in a facsimile edition reproducing all 31 brightly colored plates. Additional printed text of each poem. 64pp. 5¼ × 7.
22764-2 Pa. $3.50

PRECIOUS STONES, Max Bauer. Classic, thorough study of diamonds, rubies, emeralds, garnets, etc.: physical character, occurrence, properties, use, similar topics. 20 plates, 8 in color. 94 figures. 659pp. 6⅛ × 9¼.
21910-0, 21911-9 Pa., Two-vol. set $15.90

ENCYCLOPEDIA OF VICTORIAN NEEDLEWORK, S. F. A. Caulfeild and Blanche Saward. Full, precise descriptions of stitches, techniques for dozens of needlecrafts—most exhaustive reference of its kind. Over 800 figures. Total of 679pp. 8⅛ × 11. Two volumes. Vol. 1 22800-2 Pa. $11.95
Vol. 2 22801-0 Pa. $11.95

THE MARVELOUS LAND OF OZ, L. Frank Baum. Second Oz book, the Scarecrow and Tin Woodman are back with hero named Tip, Oz magic. 136 illustrations. 287pp. 5⅜ × 8½. 20692-0 Pa. $5.95

WILD FOWL DECOYS, Joel Barber. Basic book on the subject, by foremost authority and collector. Reveals history of decoy making and rigging, place in American culture, different kinds of decoys, how to make them, and how to use them. 140 plates. 156pp. 7⅞ × 10¾. 20011-6 Pa. $8.95

HISTORY OF LACE, Mrs. Bury Palliser. Definitive, profusely illustrated chronicle of lace from earliest times to late 19th century. Laces of Italy, Greece, England, France, Belgium, etc. Landmark of needlework scholarship. 266 illustrations. 672pp. 6⅛ × 9¼. 24742-2 Pa. $14.95

ILLUSTRATED GUIDE TO SHAKER FURNITURE, Robert Meader. All furniture and appurtenances, with much on unknown local styles. 235 photos. 146pp. 9 × 12. 22819-3 Pa. $7.95

WHALE SHIPS AND WHALING: A Pictorial Survey, George Francis Dow. Over 200 vintage engravings, drawings, photographs of barks, brigs, cutters, other vessels. Also harpoons, lances, whaling guns, many other artifacts. Comprehensive text by foremost authority. 207 black-and-white illustrations. 288pp. 6 × 9.
24808-9 Pa. $8.95

THE BERTRAMS, Anthony Trollope. Powerful portrayal of blind self-will and thwarted ambition includes one of Trollope's most heartrending love stories. 497pp. 5⅜ × 8½. 25119-5 Pa. $8.95

ADVENTURES WITH A HAND LENS, Richard Headstrom. Clearly written guide to observing and studying flowers and grasses, fish scales, moth and insect wings, egg cases, buds, feathers, seeds, leaf scars, moss, molds, ferns, common crystals, etc.—all with an ordinary, inexpensive magnifying glass. 209 exact line drawings aid in your discoveries. 220pp. 5⅜ × 8½. 23330-8 Pa. $4.50

RODIN ON ART AND ARTISTS, Auguste Rodin. Great sculptor's candid, wide-ranging comments on meaning of art; great artists; relation of sculpture to poetry, painting, music; philosophy of life, more. 76 superb black-and-white illustrations of Rodin's sculpture, drawings and prints. 119pp. 8⅜ × 11¼. 24487-3 Pa. $6.95

FIFTY CLASSIC FRENCH FILMS, 1912–1982: A Pictorial Record, Anthony Slide. Memorable stills from Grand Illusion, Beauty and the Beast, Hiroshima, Mon Amour, many more. Credits, plot synopses, reviews, etc. 160pp. 8¼ × 11.
25256-6 Pa. $11.95

THE PRINCIPLES OF PSYCHOLOGY, William James. Famous long course complete, unabridged. Stream of thought, time perception, memory, experimental methods; great work decades ahead of its time. 94 figures. 1,391pp. 5⅜ × 8½.
20381-6, 20382-4 Pa., Two-vol. set $19.90

BODIES IN A BOOKSHOP, R. T. Campbell. Challenging mystery of blackmail and murder with ingenious plot and superbly drawn characters. In the best tradition of British suspense fiction. 192pp. 5⅜ × 8½. 24720-1 Pa. $3.95

CALLAS: PORTRAIT OF A PRIMA DONNA, George Jellinek. Renowned commentator on the musical scene chronicles incredible career and life of the most controversial, fascinating, influential operatic personality of our time. 64 black-and-white photographs. 416pp. 5⅜ × 8¼. 25047-4 Pa. $7.95

GEOMETRY, RELATIVITY AND THE FOURTH DIMENSION, Rudolph Rucker. Exposition of fourth dimension, concepts of relativity as Flatland characters continue adventures. Popular, easily followed yet accurate, profound. 141 illustrations. 133pp. 5⅜ × 8½. 23400-2 Pa. $3.50

HOUSEHOLD STORIES BY THE BROTHERS GRIMM, with pictures by Walter Crane. 53 classic stories—Rumpelstiltskin, Rapunzel, Hansel and Gretel, the Fisherman and his Wife, Snow White, Tom Thumb, Sleeping Beauty, Cinderella, and so much more—lavishly illustrated with original 19th century drawings. 114 illustrations. x + 269pp. 5⅜ × 8½. 21080-4 Pa. $4.50

SUNDIALS, Albert Waugh. Far and away the best, most thorough coverage of ideas, mathematics concerned, types, construction, adjusting anywhere. Over 100 illustrations. 230pp. 5⅜ × 8½. 22947-5 Pa. $4.50

PICTURE HISTORY OF THE NORMANDIE: With 190 Illustrations, Frank O. Braynard. Full story of legendary French ocean liner: Art Deco interiors, design innovations, furnishings, celebrities, maiden voyage, tragic fire, much more. Extensive text. 144pp. 8⅞ × 11¾. 25257-4 Pa. $9.95

THE FIRST AMERICAN COOKBOOK: A Facsimile of "American Cookery," 1796, Amelia Simmons. Facsimile of the first American-written cookbook published in the United States contains authentic recipes for colonial favorites—pumpkin pudding, winter squash pudding, spruce beer, Indian slapjacks, and more. Introductory Essay and Glossary of colonial cooking terms. 80pp. 5⅜ × 8½. 24710-4 Pa. $3.50

101 PUZZLES IN THOUGHT AND LOGIC, C. R. Wylie, Jr. Solve murders and robberies, find out which fishermen are liars, how a blind man could possibly identify a color—purely by your own reasoning! 107pp. 5⅜ × 8½. 20367-0 Pa. $2.50

THE BOOK OF WORLD-FAMOUS MUSIC—CLASSICAL, POPULAR AND FOLK, James J. Fuld. Revised and enlarged republication of landmark work in musico-bibliography. Full information about nearly 1,000 songs and compositions including first lines of music and lyrics. New supplement. Index. 800pp. 5⅜ × 8¼. 24857-7 Pa. $14.95

ANTHROPOLOGY AND MODERN LIFE, Franz Boas. Great anthropologist's classic treatise on race and culture. Introduction by Ruth Bunzel. Only inexpensive paperback edition. 255pp. 5⅜ × 8½. 25245-0 Pa. $5.95

THE TALE OF PETER RABBIT, Beatrix Potter. The inimitable Peter's terrifying adventure in Mr. McGregor's garden, with all 27 wonderful, full-color Potter illustrations. 55pp. 4¼ × 5½. (Available in U.S. only) 22827-4 Pa. $1.75

THREE PROPHETIC SCIENCE FICTION NOVELS, H. G. Wells. *When the Sleeper Wakes, A Story of the Days to Come* and *The Time Machine* (full version). 335pp. 5⅜ × 8½. (Available in U.S. only) 20605-X Pa. $5.95

APICIUS COOKERY AND DINING IN IMPERIAL ROME, edited and translated by Joseph Dommers Vehling. Oldest known cookbook in existence offers readers a clear picture of what foods Romans ate, how they prepared them, etc. 49 illustrations. 301pp. 6⅛ × 9¼. 23563-7 Pa. $6.50

SHAKESPEARE LEXICON AND QUOTATION DICTIONARY, Alexander Schmidt. Full definitions, locations, shades of meaning of every word in plays and poems. More than 50,000 exact quotations. 1,485pp. 6½ × 9¼. 22726-X, 22727-8 Pa., Two-vol. set $27.90

THE WORLD'S GREAT SPEECHES, edited by Lewis Copeland and Lawrence W. Lamm. Vast collection of 278 speeches from Greeks to 1970. Powerful and effective models; unique look at history. 842pp. 5⅜ × 8½. 20468-5 Pa. $11.95

THE BLUE FAIRY BOOK, Andrew Lang. The first, most famous collection, with many familiar tales: Little Red Riding Hood, Aladdin and the Wonderful Lamp, Puss in Boots, Sleeping Beauty, Hansel and Gretel, Rumpelstiltskin; 37 in all. 138 illustrations. 390pp. 5⅜ × 8½. 21437-0 Pa. $5.95

THE STORY OF THE CHAMPIONS OF THE ROUND TABLE, Howard Pyle. Sir Launcelot, Sir Tristram and Sir Percival in spirited adventures of love and triumph retold in Pyle's inimitable style. 50 drawings, 31 full-page. xviii + 329pp. 6½ × 9¼. 21883-X Pa. $6.95

AUDUBON AND HIS JOURNALS, Maria Audubon. Unmatched two-volume portrait of the great artist, naturalist and author contains his journals, an excellent biography by his granddaughter, expert annotations by the noted ornithologist, Dr. Elliott Coues, and 37 superb illustrations. Total of 1,200pp. 5⅜ × 8.
Vol. I 25143-8 Pa. $8.95
Vol. II 25144-6 Pa. $8.95

GREAT DINOSAUR HUNTERS AND THEIR DISCOVERIES, Edwin H. Colbert. Fascinating, lavishly illustrated chronicle of dinosaur research, 1820's to 1960. Achievements of Cope, Marsh, Brown, Buckland, Mantell, Huxley, many others. 384pp. 5¼ × 8¼. 24701-5 Pa. $6.95

THE TASTEMAKERS, Russell Lynes. Informal, illustrated social history of American taste 1850's–1950's. First popularized categories Highbrow, Lowbrow, Middlebrow. 129 illustrations. New (1979) afterword. 384pp. 6 × 9.
23993-4 Pa. $6.95

DOUBLE CROSS PURPOSES, Ronald A. Knox. A treasure hunt in the Scottish Highlands, an old map, unidentified corpse, surprise discoveries keep reader guessing in this cleverly intricate tale of financial skullduggery. 2 black-and-white maps. 320pp. 5⅜ × 8½. (Available in U.S. only) 25032-6 Pa. $5.95

AUTHENTIC VICTORIAN DECORATION AND ORNAMENTATION IN FULL COLOR: 46 Plates from "Studies in Design," Christopher Dresser. Superb full-color lithographs reproduced from rare original portfolio of a major Victorian designer. 48pp. 9¼ × 12¼. 25083-0 Pa. $7.95

PRIMITIVE ART, Franz Boas. Remains the best text ever prepared on subject, thoroughly discussing Indian, African, Asian, Australian, and, especially, Northern American primitive art. Over 950 illustrations show ceramics, masks, totem poles, weapons, textiles, paintings, much more. 376pp. 5⅜ × 8. 20025-6 Pa. $6.95

SIDELIGHTS ON RELATIVITY, Albert Einstein. Unabridged republication of two lectures delivered by the great physicist in 1920–21. *Ether and Relativity* and *Geometry and Experience*. Elegant ideas in non-mathematical form, accessible to intelligent layman. vi + 56pp. 5⅜ × 8½. 24511-X Pa. $2.95

THE WIT AND HUMOR OF OSCAR WILDE, edited by Alvin Redman. More than 1,000 ripostes, paradoxes, wisecracks: Work is the curse of the drinking classes, I can resist everything except temptation, etc. 258pp. 5⅜ × 8½. 20602-5 Pa. $4.50

ADVENTURES WITH A MICROSCOPE, Richard Headstrom. 59 adventures with clothing fibers, protozoa, ferns and lichens, roots and leaves, much more. 142 illustrations. 232pp. 5⅜ × 8½. 23471-1 Pa. $3.95

PLANTS OF THE BIBLE, Harold N. Moldenke and Alma L. Moldenke. Standard reference to all 230 plants mentioned in Scriptures. Latin name, biblical reference, uses, modern identity, much more. Unsurpassed encyclopedic resource for scholars, botanists, nature lovers, students of Bible. Bibliography. Indexes. 123 black-and-white illustrations. 384pp. 6 × 9. 25069-5 Pa. $8.95

FAMOUS AMERICAN WOMEN: A Biographical Dictionary from Colonial Times to the Present, Robert McHenry, ed. From Pocahontas to Rosa Parks, 1,035 distinguished American women documented in separate biographical entries. Accurate, up-to-date data, numerous categories, spans 400 years. Indices. 493pp. 6½ × 9¼. 24523-3 Pa. $9.95

THE FABULOUS INTERIORS OF THE GREAT OCEAN LINERS IN HISTORIC PHOTOGRAPHS, William H. Miller, Jr. Some 200 superb photographs capture exquisite interiors of world's great "floating palaces"—1890's to 1980's: *Titanic, Ile de France, Queen Elizabeth, United States, Europa,* more. Approx. 200 black-and-white photographs. Captions. Text. Introduction. 160pp. 8⅜ × 11¾. 24756-2 Pa. $9.95

THE GREAT LUXURY LINERS, 1927–1954: A Photographic Record, William H. Miller, Jr. Nostalgic tribute to heyday of ocean liners. 186 photos of Ile de France, Normandie, Leviathan, Queen Elizabeth, United States, many others. Interior and exterior views. Introduction. Captions. 160pp. 9 × 12. 24056-8 Pa. $9.95

A NATURAL HISTORY OF THE DUCKS, John Charles Phillips. Great landmark of ornithology offers complete detailed coverage of nearly 200 species and subspecies of ducks: gadwall, sheldrake, merganser, pintail, many more. 74 full-color plates, 102 black-and-white. Bibliography. Total of 1,920pp. 8⅜ × 11¼. 25141-1, 25142-X Cloth. Two-vol. set $100.00

THE SEAWEED HANDBOOK: An Illustrated Guide to Seaweeds from North Carolina to Canada, Thomas F. Lee. Concise reference covers 78 species. Scientific and common names, habitat, distribution, more. Finding keys for easy identification. 224pp. 5⅜ × 8½. 25215-9 Pa. $5.95

THE TEN BOOKS OF ARCHITECTURE: The 1755 Leoni Edition, Leon Battista Alberti. Rare classic helped introduce the glories of ancient architecture to the Renaissance. 68 black-and-white plates. 336pp. 8⅜ × 11¼. 25239-6 Pa. $14.95

MISS MACKENZIE, Anthony Trollope. Minor masterpieces by Victorian master unmasks many truths about life in 19th-century England. First inexpensive edition in years. 392pp. 5⅜ × 8½. 25201-9 Pa. $7.95

THE RIME OF THE ANCIENT MARINER, Gustave Doré, Samuel Taylor Coleridge. Dramatic engravings considered by many to be his greatest work. The terrifying space of the open sea, the storms and whirlpools of an unknown ocean, the ice of Antarctica, more—all rendered in a powerful, chilling manner. Full text. 38 plates. 77pp. 9¼ × 12. 22305-1 Pa. $4.95

THE EXPEDITIONS OF ZEBULON MONTGOMERY PIKE, Zebulon Montgomery Pike. Fascinating first-hand accounts (1805–6) of exploration of Mississippi River, Indian wars, capture by Spanish dragoons, much more. 1,088pp. 5⅜ × 8½. 25254-X, 25255-8 Pa. Two-vol. set $23.90

A CONCISE HISTORY OF PHOTOGRAPHY: Third Revised Edition, Helmut Gernsheim. Best one-volume history—camera obscura, photochemistry, daguerreotypes, evolution of cameras, film, more. Also artistic aspects—landscape, portraits, fine art, etc. 281 black-and-white photographs. 26 in color. 176pp. 8⅜ × 11¼. 25128-4 Pa. $12.95

THE DORÉ BIBLE ILLUSTRATIONS, Gustave Doré. 241 detailed plates from the Bible: the Creation scenes, Adam and Eve, Flood, Babylon, battle sequences, life of Jesus, etc. Each plate is accompanied by the verses from the King James version of the Bible. 241pp. 9 × 12. 23004-X Pa. $8.95

HUGGER-MUGGER IN THE LOUVRE, Elliot Paul. Second Homer Evans mystery-comedy. Theft at the Louvre involves sleuth in hilarious, madcap caper. "A knockout."—Books. 336pp. 5⅜ × 8½. 25185-3 Pa. $5.95

FLATLAND, E. A. Abbott. Intriguing and enormously popular science-fiction classic explores the complexities of trying to survive as a two-dimensional being in a three-dimensional world. Amusingly illustrated by the author. 16 illustrations. 103pp. 5⅜ × 8½. 20001-9 Pa. $2.25

THE HISTORY OF THE LEWIS AND CLARK EXPEDITION, Meriwether Lewis and William Clark, edited by Elliott Coues. Classic edition of Lewis and Clark's day-by-day journals that later became the basis for U.S. claims to Oregon and the West. Accurate and invaluable geographical, botanical, biological, meteorological and anthropological material. Total of 1,508pp. 5⅜ × 8½. 21268-8, 21269-6, 21270-X Pa. Three-vol. set $25.50

LANGUAGE, TRUTH AND LOGIC, Alfred J. Ayer. Famous, clear introduction to Vienna, Cambridge schools of Logical Positivism. Role of philosophy, elimination of metaphysics, nature of analysis, etc. 160pp. 5⅜ × 8½. (Available in U.S. and Canada only) 20010-8 Pa. $2.95

MATHEMATICS FOR THE NONMATHEMATICIAN, Morris Kline. Detailed, college-level treatment of mathematics in cultural and historical context, with numerous exercises. For liberal arts students. Preface. Recommended Reading Lists. Tables. Index. Numerous black-and-white figures. xvi + 641pp. 5⅜ × 8½. 24823-2 Pa. $11.95

28 SCIENCE FICTION STORIES, H. G. Wells. Novels, *Star Begotten* and *Men Like Gods,* plus 26 short stories: "Empire of the Ants," "A Story of the Stone Age," "The Stolen Bacillus," "In the Abyss," etc. 915pp. 5⅜ × 8½. (Available in U.S. only) 20265-8 Cloth. $10.95

HANDBOOK OF PICTORIAL SYMBOLS, Rudolph Modley. 3,250 signs and symbols, many systems in full; official or heavy commercial use. Arranged by subject. Most in Pictorial Archive series. 143pp. 8⅛ × 11. 23357-X Pa. $5.95

INCIDENTS OF TRAVEL IN YUCATAN, John L. Stephens. Classic (1843) exploration of jungles of Yucatan, looking for evidences of Maya civilization. Travel adventures, Mexican and Indian culture, etc. Total of 669pp. 5⅜ × 8½. 20926-1, 20927-X Pa., Two-vol. set $9.90

DEGAS: An Intimate Portrait, Ambroise Vollard. Charming, anecdotal memoir by famous art dealer of one of the greatest 19th-century French painters. 14 black-and-white illustrations. Introduction by Harold L. Van Doren. 96pp. 5⅜ × 8½.
25131-4 Pa. $3.95

PERSONAL NARRATIVE OF A PILGRIMAGE TO ALMANDINAH AND MECCAH, Richard Burton. Great travel classic by remarkably colorful personality. Burton, disguised as a Moroccan, visited sacred shrines of Islam, narrowly escaping death. 47 illustrations. 959pp. 5⅜ × 8½.   21217-3, 21218-1 Pa., Two-vol. set $17.90

PHRASE AND WORD ORIGINS, A. H. Holt. Entertaining, reliable, modern study of more than 1,200 colorful words, phrases, origins and histories. Much unexpected information. 254pp. 5⅜ × 8½.   20758-7 Pa. $5.95

THE RED THUMB MARK, R. Austin Freeman. In this first Dr. Thorndyke case, the great scientific detective draws fascinating conclusions from the nature of a single fingerprint. Exciting story, authentic science. 320pp. 5⅜ × 8½. (Available in U.S. only)   25210-8 Pa. $5.95

AN EGYPTIAN HIEROGLYPHIC DICTIONARY, E. A. Wallis Budge. Monumental work containing about 25,000 words or terms that occur in texts ranging from 3000 B.C. to 600 A.D. Each entry consists of a transliteration of the word, the word in hieroglyphs, and the meaning in English. 1,314pp. 6⅜ × 10.
23615-3, 23616-1 Pa., Two-vol. set $27.90

THE COMPLEAT STRATEGYST: Being a Primer on the Theory of Games of Strategy, J. D. Williams. Highly entertaining classic describes, with many illustrated examples, how to select best strategies in conflict situations. Prefaces. Appendices. xvi + 268pp. 5⅜ × 8½.   25101-2 Pa. $5.95

THE ROAD TO OZ, L. Frank Baum. Dorothy meets the Shaggy Man, little Button-Bright and the Rainbow's beautiful daughter in this delightful trip to the magical Land of Oz. 272pp. 5⅜ × 8.   25208-6 Pa. $4.95

POINT AND LINE TO PLANE, Wassily Kandinsky. Seminal exposition of role of point, line, other elements in non-objective painting. Essential to understanding 20th-century art. 127 illustrations. 192pp. 6½ × 9¼.   23808-3 Pa. $4.50

LADY ANNA, Anthony Trollope. Moving chronicle of Countess Lovel's bitter struggle to win for herself and daughter Anna their rightful rank and fortune— perhaps at cost of sanity itself. 384pp. 5⅜ × 8½.   24669-8 Pa. $6.95

EGYPTIAN MAGIC, E. A. Wallis Budge. Sums up all that is known about magic in Ancient Egypt: the role of magic in controlling the gods, powerful amulets that warded off evil spirits, scarabs of immortality, use of wax images, formulas and spells, the secret name, much more. 253pp. 5⅜ × 8½.   22681-6 Pa. $4.50

THE DANCE OF SIVA, Ananda Coomaraswamy. Preeminent authority unfolds the vast metaphysic of India: the revelation of her art, conception of the universe, social organization, etc. 27 reproductions of art masterpieces. 192pp. 5⅜ × 8½.
24817-8 Pa. $5.95

CHRISTMAS CUSTOMS AND TRADITIONS, Clement A. Miles. Origin, evolution, significance of religious, secular practices. Caroling, gifts, yule logs, much more. Full, scholarly yet fascinating; non-sectarian. 400pp. 5⅜ × 8½.
23354-5 Pa. $6.50

THE HUMAN FIGURE IN MOTION, Eadweard Muybridge. More than 4,500 stopped-action photos, in action series, showing undraped men, women, children jumping, lying down, throwing, sitting, wrestling, carrying, etc. 390pp. 7⅞ × 10⅝.
20204-6 Cloth. $19.95

THE MAN WHO WAS THURSDAY, Gilbert Keith Chesterton. Witty, fast-paced novel about a club of anarchists in turn-of-the-century London. Brilliant social, religious, philosophical speculations. 128pp. 5⅜ × 8½.
25121-7 Pa. $3.95

A CEZANNE SKETCHBOOK: Figures, Portraits, Landscapes and Still Lifes, Paul Cezanne. Great artist experiments with tonal effects, light, mass, other qualities in over 100 drawings. A revealing view of developing master painter, precursor of Cubism. 102 black-and-white illustrations. 144pp. 8¾ × 6⅜.
24790-2 Pa. $5.95

AN ENCYCLOPEDIA OF BATTLES: Accounts of Over 1,560 Battles from 1479 B.C. to the Present, David Eggenberger. Presents essential details of every major battle in recorded history, from the first battle of Megiddo in 1479 B.C. to Grenada in 1984. List of Battle Maps. New Appendix covering the years 1967–1984. Index. 99 illustrations. 544pp. 6½ × 9¼.
24913-1 Pa. $14.95

AN ETYMOLOGICAL DICTIONARY OF MODERN ENGLISH, Ernest Weekley. Richest, fullest work, by foremost British lexicographer. Detailed word histories. Inexhaustible. Total of 856pp. 6½ × 9¼.
21873-2, 21874-0 Pa., Two-vol. set $17.00

WEBSTER'S AMERICAN MILITARY BIOGRAPHIES, edited by Robert McHenry. Over 1,000 figures who shaped 3 centuries of American military history. Detailed biographies of Nathan Hale, Douglas MacArthur, Mary Hallaren, others. Chronologies of engagements, more. Introduction. Addenda. 1,033 entries in alphabetical order. xi + 548pp. 6½ × 9¼. (Available in U.S. only)
24758-9 Pa. $11.95

LIFE IN ANCIENT EGYPT, Adolf Erman. Detailed older account, with much not in more recent books: domestic life, religion, magic, medicine, commerce, and whatever else needed for complete picture. Many illustrations. 597pp. 5⅜ × 8½.
22632-8 Pa. $8.95

HISTORIC COSTUME IN PICTURES, Braun & Schneider. Over 1,450 costumed figures shown, covering a wide variety of peoples: kings, emperors, nobles, priests, servants, soldiers, scholars, townsfolk, peasants, merchants, courtiers, cavaliers, and more. 256pp. 8⅜ × 11¼.
23150-X Pa. $7.95

THE NOTEBOOKS OF LEONARDO DA VINCI, edited by J. P. Richter. Extracts from manuscripts reveal great genius; on painting, sculpture, anatomy, sciences, geography, etc. Both Italian and English. 186 ms. pages reproduced, plus 500 additional drawings, including studies for *Last Supper, Sforza* monument, etc. 860pp. 7⅞ × 10¾. (Available in U.S. only) 22572-0, 22573-9 Pa., Two-vol. set $25.90

THE ART NOUVEAU STYLE BOOK OF ALPHONSE MUCHA: All 72 Plates from "Documents Decoratifs" in Original Color, Alphonse Mucha. Rare copyright-free design portfolio by high priest of Art Nouveau. Jewelry, wallpaper, stained glass, furniture, figure studies, plant and animal motifs, etc. Only complete one-volume edition. 80pp. 9⅜ × 12¼. 24044-4 Pa. $8.95

ANIMALS: 1,419 COPYRIGHT-FREE ILLUSTRATIONS OF MAMMALS, BIRDS, FISH, INSECTS, ETC., edited by Jim Harter. Clear wood engravings present, in extremely lifelike poses, over 1,000 species of animals. One of the most extensive pictorial sourcebooks of its kind. Captions. Index. 284pp. 9 × 12.
23766-4 Pa. $9.95

OBELISTS FLY HIGH, C. Daly King. Masterpiece of American detective fiction, long out of print, involves murder on a 1935 transcontinental flight—"a very thrilling story"—NY Times. Unabridged and unaltered republication of the edition published by William Collins Sons & Co. Ltd., London, 1935. 288pp. 5⅜ × 8½. (Available in U.S. only) 25036-9 Pa. $4.95

VICTORIAN AND EDWARDIAN FASHION: A Photographic Survey, Alison Gernsheim. First fashion history completely illustrated by contemporary photographs. Full text plus 235 photos, 1840–1914, in which many celebrities appear. 240pp. 6½ × 9¼. 24205-6 Pa. $6.00

THE ART OF THE FRENCH ILLUSTRATED BOOK, 1700–1914, Gordon N. Ray. Over 630 superb book illustrations by Fragonard, Delacroix, Daumier, Doré, Grandville, Manet, Mucha, Steinlen, Toulouse-Lautrec and many others. Preface. Introduction. 633 halftones. Indices of artists, authors & titles, binders and provenances. Appendices. Bibliography. 608pp. 8⅜ × 11¼. 25086-5 Pa. $24.95

THE WONDERFUL WIZARD OF OZ, L. Frank Baum. Facsimile in full color of America's finest children's classic. 143 illustrations by W. W. Denslow. 267pp. 5⅜ × 8½. 20691-2 Pa. $5.95

FRONTIERS OF MODERN PHYSICS: New Perspectives on Cosmology, Relativity, Black Holes and Extraterrestrial Intelligence, Tony Rothman, et al. For the intelligent layman. Subjects include: cosmological models of the universe; black holes; the neutrino; the search for extraterrestrial intelligence. Introduction. 46 black-and-white illustrations. 192pp. 5⅜ × 8½. 24587-X Pa. $6.95

THE FRIENDLY STARS, Martha Evans Martin & Donald Howard Menzel. Classic text marshalls the stars together in an engaging, non-technical survey, presenting them as sources of beauty in night sky. 23 illustrations. Foreword. 2 star charts. Index. 147pp. 5⅜ × 8½. 21099-5 Pa. $3.50

FADS AND FALLACIES IN THE NAME OF SCIENCE, Martin Gardner. Fair, witty appraisal of cranks, quacks, and quackeries of science and pseudoscience: hollow earth, Velikovsky, orgone energy, Dianetics, flying saucers, Bridey Murphy, food and medical fads, etc. Revised, expanded In the Name of Science. "A very able and even-tempered presentation."—The New Yorker. 363pp. 5⅜ × 8.
20394-8 Pa. $6.50

ANCIENT EGYPT: ITS CULTURE AND HISTORY, J. E Manchip White. From pre-dynastics through Ptolemies: society, history, political structure, religion, daily life, literature, cultural heritage. 48 plates. 217pp. 5⅜ × 8½. 22548-8 Pa. $4.95

SIR HARRY HOTSPUR OF HUMBLETHWAITE, Anthony Trollope. Incisive, unconventional psychological study of a conflict between a wealthy baronet, his idealistic daughter, and their scapegrace cousin. The 1870 novel in its first inexpensive edition in years. 250pp. 5⅜ × 8½. 24953-0 Pa. $5.95

LASERS AND HOLOGRAPHY, Winston E. Kock. Sound introduction to burgeoning field, expanded (1981) for second edition. Wave patterns, coherence, lasers, diffraction, zone plates, properties of holograms, recent advances. 84 illustrations. 160pp. 5⅜ × 8¼. (Except in United Kingdom) 24041-X Pa. $3.50

INTRODUCTION TO ARTIFICIAL INTELLIGENCE: SECOND, EN-LARGED EDITION, Philip C. Jackson, Jr. Comprehensive survey of artificial intelligence—the study of how machines (computers) can be made to act intelligently. Includes introductory and advanced material. Extensive notes updating the main text. 132 black-and-white illustrations. 512pp. 5⅜ × 8½. 24864-X Pa. $8.95

HISTORY OF INDIAN AND INDONESIAN ART, Ananda K. Coomaraswamy. Over 400 illustrations illuminate classic study of Indian art from earliest Harappa finds to early 20th century. Provides philosophical, religious and social insights. 304pp. 6⅛ × 9⅜. 25005-9 Pa. $8.95

THE GOLEM, Gustav Meyrink. Most famous supernatural novel in modern European literature, set in Ghetto of Old Prague around 1890. Compelling story of mystical experiences, strange transformations, profound terror. 13 black-and-white illustrations. 224pp. 5⅜ × 8½. (Available in U.S. only) 25025-3 Pa. $5.95

ARMADALE, Wilkie Collins. Third great mystery novel by the author of *The Woman in White* and *The Moonstone*. Original magazine version with 40 illustrations. 597pp. 5⅜ × 8½. 23429-0 Pa. $9.95

PICTORIAL ENCYCLOPEDIA OF HISTORIC ARCHITECTURAL PLANS, DETAILS AND ELEMENTS: With 1,880 Line Drawings of Arches, Domes, Doorways, Facades, Gables, Windows, etc., John Theodore Haneman. Sourcebook of inspiration for architects, designers, others. Bibliography. Captions. 141pp. 9 × 12. 24605-1 Pa. $6.95

BENCHLEY LOST AND FOUND, Robert Benchley. Finest humor from early 30's, about pet peeves, child psychologists, post office and others. Mostly unavailable elsewhere. 73 illustrations by Peter Arno and others. 183pp. 5⅜ × 8½. 22410-4 Pa. $3.95

ERTÉ GRAPHICS, Erté. Collection of striking color graphics: *Seasons, Alphabet, Numerals, Aces* and *Precious Stones*. 50 plates, including 4 on covers. 48pp. 9⅜ × 12¼. 23580-7 Pa. $6.95

THE JOURNAL OF HENRY D. THOREAU, edited by Bradford Torrey, F. H. Allen. Complete reprinting of 14 volumes, 1837–61, over two million words; the sourcebooks for *Walden*, etc. Definitive. All original sketches, plus 75 photographs. 1,804pp. 8½ × 12¼. 20312-3, 20313-1 Cloth., Two-vol. set $80.00

CASTLES: THEIR CONSTRUCTION AND HISTORY, Sidney Toy. Traces castle development from ancient roots. Nearly 200 photographs and drawings illustrate moats, keeps, baileys, many other features. Caernarvon, Dover Castles, Hadrian's Wall, Tower of London, dozens more. 256pp. 5⅜ × 8¼. 24898-4 Pa. $5.95

AMERICAN CLIPPER SHIPS: 1833–1858, Octavius T. Howe & Frederick C. Matthews. Fully-illustrated, encyclopedic review of 352 clipper ships from the period of America's greatest maritime supremacy. Introduction. 109 halftones. 5 black-and-white line illustrations. Index. Total of 928pp. 5⅜ × 8½.
25115-2, 25116-0 Pa., Two-vol. set $17.90

TOWARDS A NEW ARCHITECTURE, Le Corbusier. Pioneering manifesto by great architect, near legendary founder of "International School." Technical and aesthetic theories, views on industry, economics, relation of form to function, "mass-production spirit," much more. Profusely illustrated. Unabridged translation of 13th French edition. Introduction by Frederick Etchells. 320pp. 6⅛ × 9¼. (Available in U.S. only)
25023-7 Pa. $8.95

THE BOOK OF KELLS, edited by Blanche Cirker. Inexpensive collection of 32 full-color, full-page plates from the greatest illuminated manuscript of the Middle Ages, painstakingly reproduced from rare facsimile edition. Publisher's Note. Captions. 32pp. 9⅜ × 12¼.
24345-1 Pa. $4.95

BEST SCIENCE FICTION STORIES OF H. G. WELLS, H. G. Wells. Full novel *The Invisible Man*, plus 17 short stories: "The Crystal Egg," "Aepyornis Island," "The Strange Orchid," etc. 303pp. 5⅜ × 8½. (Available in U.S. only)
21531-8 Pa. $4.95

AMERICAN SAILING SHIPS: Their Plans and History, Charles G. Davis. Photos, construction details of schooners, frigates, clippers, other sailcraft of 18th to early 20th centuries—plus entertaining discourse on design, rigging, nautical lore, much more. 137 black-and-white illustrations. 240pp. 6⅛ × 9¼.
24658-2 Pa. $5.95

ENTERTAINING MATHEMATICAL PUZZLES, Martin Gardner. Selection of author's favorite conundrums involving arithmetic, money, speed, etc., with lively commentary. Complete solutions. 112pp. 5⅜ × 8½.
25211-6 Pa. $2.95

THE WILL TO BELIEVE, HUMAN IMMORTALITY, William James. Two books bound together. Effect of irrational on logical, and arguments for human immortality. 402pp. 5⅜ × 8½.
20291-7 Pa. $7.50

THE HAUNTED MONASTERY and THE CHINESE MAZE MURDERS, Robert Van Gulik. 2 full novels by Van Gulik continue adventures of Judge Dee and his companions. An evil Taoist monastery, seemingly supernatural events; overgrown topiary maze that hides strange crimes. Set in 7th-century China. 27 illustrations. 328pp. 5⅜ × 8½.
23502-5 Pa. $5.95

CELEBRATED CASES OF JUDGE DEE (DEE GOONG AN), translated by Robert Van Gulik. Authentic 18th-century Chinese detective novel; Dee and associates solve three interlocked cases. Led to Van Gulik's own stories with same characters. Extensive introduction. 9 illustrations. 237pp. 5⅜ × 8½.
23337-5 Pa. $4.95

Prices subject to change without notice.

Available at your book dealer or write for free catalog to Dept. GI, Dover Publications, Inc., 31 East 2nd St., Mineola, N.Y. 11501. Dover publishes more than 175 books each year on science, elementary and advanced mathematics, biology, music, art, literary history, social sciences and other areas.